The Passive Programming Playbook

The Passive Programming Playbook

101 Ways to Get Library Customers off the Sidelines

Paula Willey and Andria L. Amaral

Copyright © 2021 by Paula Willey and Andria L. Amaral

Library of Congress Cataloging-in-Publication Data

Names: Willey, Paula, author. | Amaral, Andria L., author.
Title: The passive programming playbook : 101 ways to get library customers
   off the sidelines / Paula Willey and Andria L. Amaral.
Description: Santa Barbara, California : Libraries Unlimited, an imprint of
   ABC-CLIO, LLC, [2021] | Includes bibliographical references and index.
Identifiers: LCCN 2021007454 (print) | LCCN 2021007455 (ebook) | ISBN
   9781440870569 (paperback) | ISBN 9781440870576 (ebook)
Subjects: LCSH: Libraries—Activity programs—United States. | BISAC:
   LANGUAGE ARTS & DISCIPLINES / Library & Information Science / General
Classification: LCC Z716.33 .W545 2021 (print) | LCC Z716.33 (ebook) |
   DDC 025.5—dc23
LC record available at https://lccn.loc.gov/2021007454
LC ebook record available at https://lccn.loc.gov/2021007455

ISBN: 978-1-4408-7056-9 (print)
      978-1-4408-7057-6 (ebook)

25 24 23 22 21   1 2 3 4 5

This book is also available as an eBook.

Libraries Unlimited
An Imprint of ABC-CLIO, LLC

ABC-CLIO, LLC
147 Castilian Drive
Santa Barbara, California 93117
www.abc-clio.com

This book is printed on acid-free paper ∞

Manufactured in the United States of America

Contents

Acknowledgments

Andria remembers her favorite library school professor, Dr. Pat Feehan, saying that "when librarians steal, we do it with both hands." (Note: Dr. Pat has no recollection of saying this, but Andria's been reciting the quote for decades, and as Dr. Pat taught Andria everything she knows about programming, we're running with it.) For the past several years, we have been the weird adults prowling through your library, snapping pictures of your trivia posters, library pets, and writing prompts. Sorry if we startled you. But your ideas are too good not to share.

We've made every effort to track down and credit individuals and libraries for the ideas we've adapted, adopted, or just reproduced outright. But a lot of ideas develop similarly in different places—call it convergent evolution for library programming—so we apologize if you see something that looks familiar and don't see yourself credited.

Other ideas came from Facebook groups, from conversations at professional conferences, and from colleagues who knew we were collecting cool passive programs. We owe you all a tremendous debt.

We both want to thank our coworkers who have good-naturedly endured all the wacky ideas we test-drove on the road to writing this book, and who diligently counted all the slips in the jars, the comments on the whiteboards, and the sticker dots on the polls to help quantify our passive programs' success. And most of all, we are grateful to our customers, who inspire us to create opportunities for them to learn, explore, and grow in our libraries.

Introduction

Libraries always seem to be short on resources. If we're not understaffed, we're short on space. If we have plenty of space, we've got no budget. Maybe we're low on all three. Even if you work in library paradise—a spacious, fully staffed facility with a luxurious budget (it has to exist, right?)—you are still probably not interacting with every person who walks in the door.

This is where passive programming comes in.

In this book, you'll find ways to make mountainous program stats out of molehill budgets. You'll learn how to squeeze program prep into stray seconds (OK, minutes) of staff time. And you'll get great advice on how to wedge an additional program or activity into the most miniscule unused space—a shelf, ten inches of desk space, even the air above your head.

Passive programming isn't meant to replace library-led programs. Instead, it's a great way to further enrich your imaginative, rich, active program schedule and even leverage it into additional interactions with customers.

We can't even count the number of ideas we've included here (we stopped counting once we got to 101), and we've only scratched the surface of what resourceful library staff around the world dream up for their customers. You might have something going on right now that we've never even thought of. Share it! Post it to Pinterest, Instagram, Twitter, or a library Facebook group and use the hashtag #passiveprogramming so that we all can steal it.

Giving customers opportunities to engage and express themselves results in priceless interactions that will brighten your day, stave off burnout, and motivate you to do even more passive programming. At the end of each chapter, you'll find "instant replays" of some of the true hilarious and touching moments we've experienced. We hope they inspire you.

A note on booklists and examples: you'll find booklists and sample quiz questions for many of the programs in this book. However, in other places, we've elected not to include them. Our rule of thumb is if it took us more than half an hour to gather a list, we put it in the book. If it's something that most library folks will be able to put together with a minimum of shelf scanning or internet searching, we left it out.

Have fun!

Paula and Andria

Part I

Rules, Equipment, and Keeping Score

1

Step Up Your Game: Why You Need Passive Programming in Your Library

Passive programming, simply put, is a way to engage your library customers at their own pace and interest level through self-directed activities. Amy Koester and Marge Loch-Wouters call it "unprogramming" (showmelibrarian. blogspot.com/2013/07). Megan Emery Schadlich refers to it as "antiprogramming" in her book *Cooking Up Library Programs Teens and 'Tweens Will Love*. In her books on "teen programs that work," RoseMary Honnold calls them "independent programs," and Susannah Richards of Eastern Connecticut State University prefers the term "environmental engagement."

Call it what you will, these available anytime independent activities all amount to the same thing: adding value to your customers' library visits and creating opportunities for them to engage and interact with staff, other library users, and your materials and services.

We can't be everywhere at once. Therefore, we need to optimize our environment so that every customer comes away entertained or informed. Or, ideally, both. This can be as minimal as a bulletin board with a match game or can be as elaborate as Prereader Circuit Training.

It's also great for people who just really want to slink in and slink out and really don't want to talk to people (*raises hand). Librarians are great at the peppy thing in our professional life, but a whole lot of us are just not the join-in type. So we have great empathy for the recalcitrant, slightly shy patron.

A word about stealing: we all *have* jobs. Nobody has time to invent new stuff every day. So we're giving you a whole book full of fantastic ideas with permission to steal, adapt, and make them your own. You're welcome.

Passive programming is a starting point

Passive programming is not a goal in and of itself. Done right, it's an ongoing first step to build your audience and establish relationships with your customers. Passive programming doesn't mean you get to just sit back, put your feet up on the desk, and let it happen. You're keeping an eye on it, adjusting it to create more appeal or add more value, and evaluating its effectiveness every day. In addition, passive programming creates opportunities for further engagement, and it's up to you to take advantage of those moments and bring the transaction to the next level.

Your whiteboard asks people to write "the farthest place they've ever traveled"—and you notice a teen girl has written "Prague." That's your cue to ask her about her travels and maybe booktalk *The Daughter of Smoke and Bone* by Laini Taylor. Passive programming is also a great way to get to know the names of your customers. Once you do, the simple act of smiling and greeting someone by name when they walk into your area makes them feel seen and does so much to establish you and your space as warm and welcoming.

Passive programming is good for your budget

Passive programming will help stretch your programming budget while increasing your programming statistics and improve your overall ratio of participants to dollars spent. If you spent $100 on a program that only 20 people attended, but 50 people participated in your passive program that only cost a few office supplies and 20 minutes of staff time, then overall you've spent well under a buck per program participant that month.

This makes administrators happy and looks great on your bottom line.

Passive programming is good for your stats

How do you make the case for more supplies, more equipment, more staff? Demonstrate that you are reaching tons of people, even given your meager resources. Your overall program participation numbers present a powerful negotiation tool—an easily understood metric that reflects engagement—and passive programs are an easy, cost-effective way to drive that number up. In our chapter on statistics and sharing, we will examine different ways to keep and use this data.

Passive programming is perfect for teens

For those working with young adults, passive programming is essential. If you are just starting a Young Adult department, passive programming is the best way to build your audience, get to know your regulars, and learn what interests them.

Teens are notoriously difficult to plan programs for: many of them have lives that are already so filled with homework, jobs, and after-school activities that they have little interest in attending any program that feels too much like school (no surprise there, they already spend seven hours a day in a forced learning environment). In addition, teens in suburban and rural areas are rarely in control of their transportation, so even if they are interested in a program and have the free time, they may not be able to get there on the scheduled day.

Plus, the very nature of adolescence predisposes them to distrust adults and bristle at being told what to do and when to do it. Self-directed activities allow them the freedom to develop and discover their own interests and talents. And isn't that one of the goals of public libraries, to encourage curiosity and self-education?

Besides, teenagers are scary and weird. That's just science. Surly or monosyllabic is a legit developmental stage for some kids. But they're still in there, and passive programming, done right, can help break through their uncertainty and posturing by giving them a way to engage with staff in a nonthreatening way. This facilitates getting to know them on a laid-back, individual level, and once a teen recognizes that you are truly interested in them, and you start to learn what makes them tick, they become a lot less scary and weird (and so do you).

A successful teen space should have a variety of self-directed activities with which teens can engage at their own pace and interest level. For so many young adults, the hour or so they spend hanging out at the library after school is the only unstructured time they have in their lives; take that opportunity to provide optional activities that encourage exploration, literacy, and creativity.

Passive programming is ideal for adults

Adult programming is tricky, too. Most people know libraries offer programs for children, but many don't even realize we also have them for adults. And grownups in general are more discerning than little kids are in terms of the types of activities they're willing to try. If an adult has attempted knitting twice already without success, they're not likely to be tempted into the library for a knit and crochet program.

Adult time is generally more precious as well. Although you might want to learn how to compost, you just don't have time to attend the library's gardening program with all your work and household responsibilities. Or maybe you have the time, but only on Sunday afternoon after the grocery shopping, and that's not when the program is offered. Or you plan to attend, but life gets in the way.

Many adult services librarians we've talked to are looking to passive programming to get adults engaged with the library. Contributing a thought to a kindness wall or voting in a favorite candy poll exerts a negligible time burden on a busy schedule, but it converts a drop-off/pickup visit into an interaction. It may elicit a smile or a brief warm feeling, and these tiny interactions have a cumulative effect.

Next time that customer is in the library, she'll stop to read the kind thoughts of others or check in on the results of the poll. This pause leads to a brief staff interaction: "Who voted for circus peanuts? Gross, right?" What other fun little extras can you find at the library? Oh look, they have a gardening program!

Passive programming creates community

For all ages, passive programming welcomes, supports, and engages customers who might not otherwise see themselves in the library or feel welcome at events: people who are non-neurotypical or disabled, new arrivals from other countries, or people with social or economic disadvantages. It's an easy way to provide people with the sense of belonging and community that's key to emotional well-being. Introverts, English language learners, and others who may be reluctant or feel unable to engage with staff are invited to contribute a drawing or an opinion that they may share at their own pace and without stress or judgment.

Also, someone who thinks they're the only person in the world who likes circus peanuts may see your candy poll and realize they're not alone.

Passive programming is inclusive

It can happen anytime

Few things are more demoralizing to library staff than going through the effort of planning a special library event and having a disappointing turnout. We've all been there. Even the most interesting and valuable program can fail to draw a crowd because of scheduling conflicts, bad weather, or inadequate promotion.

Passive programs eliminate those barriers by being available whenever the customer is in the library, allowing them to interact and feel part of their community without having to try and fit another event into their already over-scheduled lives. Everyone has the opportunity to participate, regardless of the day or time of their visit.

It accommodates all abilities

In addition, passive programs are self-paced. Customers can spend as little or as much time as they want working on writing or drawing prompts, creating blackout poetry, or decorating their contribution to your Dream Mobile. This takes the pressure out of programming for families with little children and customers who may need extra time to complete an activity. And the very nature of passive programming makes it a perfect fit for anyone with a short attention span!

It takes advantage of downtime

When you have an entire kindergarten class waiting to sign up for summer reading, have themed passive programming available. In areas where caregivers lounge around, playing with their babies and toddlers, make sure you have instructions and information about reading readiness activities close at hand. Do you often see parents or children cooling their heels near the computers while their kids or parents do work? These are all excellent opportunities to add value to the library visit, to teach without lecturing, and to make your customers feel like their needs are not only being addressed but anticipated.

It lets you run concurrent programs for customers of all ages

For parents who may think of the library as just a place to bring their children for story time, adult passive programs can provide a window into all the other resources we provide and give them an opportunity for self-expression. And other family members who may have been dragged along to events (grumpy older siblings, impatient youngsters, babysitting grandparents) will also have an opportunity to experience a new side to the library by engaging in these activities.

Passive programming extends existing programming

Passive programs in the children's department add value to your story times and puppet shows by encouraging families to stick around after the event to engage with other activities that also foster early literacy and learning. Supplying attendees of adult or teen programs with a craft or writing prompt that ties in with the subject of the program encourages them to linger in the library and learn more. And if you count passive program participation on the top of program attendance, boom—you just doubled your statistics for the day. Good job!

You can also use passive programs to prep for active programs or to flesh them out. When you ask customers to write their Black History Month hero on your whiteboard, for example, you end up with a list of people to feature when you're making hero collages. At Paula's library, we made buildings out of cardboard boxes to create a neighborhood display. This cardboard community really came to life when we added the two-dimensional streetscapes that people drew on the roll paper we left out on the craft table as a drive-by art project.

Passive programs can also be used to promote upcoming events. At Andria's library, Harry Potter–themed passive programs like tabletop Quidditch fill the week leading up to a Friday night after-hours festival, "Hogwarts after Dark." Flyers advertising the program are posted nearby, and whenever we see someone interacting with one of these activities, we invite them to join us at the big event.

Passive programming is adaptable

Once you get in the habit of thinking "passively," you will be able to create a self-directed activity to fit any given theme. This is your secret weapon when you're asked to program around a certain subject and can't come up with anything that you or your audience will find appealing. Did your supervisor assign you the task of creating a teen program for Money Smart Week? Instead of holding a Financial Literacy for Teens workshop and hoping young adults show up for it (and let's be honest, they likely won't unless their parents force them), why not offer a variety of activities inspired by the Saturday Shopping method you'll find in our chapter on a week of passive programming? You will reach more people with less stress and expense and have a much better chance to achieve your goal of helping young people learn how to manage their money.

Passive programming sends literacy activities home

Most parents are eager to learn how they can support the academic success of their children and encourage a love of learning. Reading Passport programs like 1000 Books before Kindergarten give them a blueprint to follow and help develop good reading habits (and ensure return visits to the library).

When you set out a stack of activity sheets, some customers will take extra to bring home for other family members to complete. Though this doesn't "count" as official program participation for statistical purposes, it promotes community literacy and literally brings home the message that the library has lots to offer.

Passive programming meets strategic goals

Most, if not all, of the seemingly fun and frivolous activities in this book have surreptitious skill-building components and are outcome based. They help meet developmental needs, promote literacy, raise awareness of library services and collections, and foster community connections. We highlight these outcomes throughout, but it is worth noting just a few activities whose value has been validated by recent research.

- Drawing and sketching promotes long-term memory (Fernandes et al., 2018)
- Choice and agency support engagement (Gronneberg and Johnston, 2015)
- Moving and learning (Peterson et al., 2014). Circuit-training activities and engagement with the library's outside spaces satisfy kinetic learners.
- Students have a greater need than ever for quiet, reflective spaces such as the Chill Corner we describe in our chapter on Special Spaces (Barrett et al., 2015)

Passive programming invites expression

After a crisis in your community, passive programming can help people come together, process difficult emotions, and heal. After the 2017 wildfires in California, customers of the Napa Library shared their stories and frustrations on a giant whiteboard with daily prompts and were invited to write or draw their memories and emotions. These stories and drawings were bound in a volume that is now in their permanent collection.

After the Mother Emanuel church shooting devastated the Charleston community in 2015, memory books were placed in each library branch, giving residents a place to express their grief and leave messages for the lives that were lost. Later, as the community moved toward healing and positivity, staff created a selfie station in the Main library lobby with the prompt: "I make a difference by:" and a small whiteboard on which visitors could answer the question and pose for a photo to be added to the display.

Even a simple whiteboard prompt like "What fictional universe would you most want to live in?" or "What's your superpower?" encourages customers to think about and share the ways they define themselves.

Passive programming enhances partnerships

A monthlong passive program, sponsored by a community partner, can provide that partner with much more visibility and reach than a one-and-done event. This can lead to bigger partnerships and more support in the future. Maybe a local restaurant will sponsor your Blind Date with a Book activity: signage and "rate your date" entry slips would be branded with their logo and displayed all month; in exchange, they donate a gift card for a free dinner for two to give away as a prize.

If a local business or organization proposes a partnership, and there's no obvious way to implement one, flip through this book, find a passive program idea, and make it work!

Passive programming improves outreach

Setting up a table or booth at a community festival, farmers' market, or school literacy night is a fantastic way to reach new customers and tell them about everything your library offers. But that only works if people actually stop at your booth. Draw them over with an eye-catching passive program that encourages them to stop for a moment; contribute a thought or idea and read other responses; and then hit them with your calendar of events, reading lists, library card applications, and assorted pamphlets.

Passive programming changes minds

Older adults who still view libraries as quiet book depositories are introduced to the concept of public libraries as interactive community centers. Teens who feel invisible or unheard are empowered and given a voice. Children who think librarians are mean or uptight learn differently when they make one laugh by reading them a fart joke and are told a joke in return. Anyone who thinks libraries are obsolete in the age of Google gets a crash course on all that the library has to offer.

The simple act of participating in a passive program, whether it's adding a vote to a poll or successfully completing a word search, creates a small but potent rush of positive emotion that leaves customers feeling good about the library and more likely to return—a vital first step in building a community of dedicated library users.

What passive programming ISN'T*

Book displays
Bulletin boards
Bookmarks
Newsletters

Except when it is

*UNLESS: you add an interactive element. Passive programming is a two-way street. There has to be a way for the customer to engage meaningfully.

A bookmark becomes a passive program if it is placed inside a book at checkout and has space where the customer can rate the book, write comments, and return to the library as entry to a raffle. If your Women's History bulletin board has a place for visitors to contribute the names of women who inspire them, it is transformed from an information source to a passive program. A Poetry Month book display becomes interactive if you leave out a pile of pages from deleted books and invite customers to create and post blackout poetry on a nearby wall or corkboard.

What about spaces and equipment?

Is a Makerspace a passive program? What about toys, puzzles, board games, and art supplies? How about LEGO? Some libraries call train tables, puppet theaters, and the like "passive activities." We find that kind of a contradiction in terms—let's just call them help-yourself interaction areas.

But do they "count"? In a way, it depends what you do with them. Technically these are self-directed activities, and if you quantify their use, you can count them as passive programs. However, to really exercise your customers' STEAM skills and make the experience memorable and enriching, ideally you will go one step beyond just setting out supplies, opening the door to the Makerspace, and sitting back to let the magic happen.

Create a monthly Maker Challenge for visitors to your Makerspace. Put a timer next to the LEGO and offer builders a reward for doing a timed build. Assemble identical sets of bricks in a zip-top bag with a slip that asks, "What Can You Make with These 100 Pieces?" Post a monthly theme or prompt next to your art supplies to inspire your artists—build a display or a contest around the results.

Some people need guidance and ideas to spark their creativity. When you ask people to stretch their abilities and follow directions, when they can compare results with others or enter their creation in a contest, that's undeniably programming, whether staff is there to guide it or not. You'll find inspiration in our chapter with ideas for anytime.

And absolutely, you want to have tabletop games and jigsaw puzzles available for in-house customer use, because those are definitely means of engagement and add value to the library experience, but they are not the point of this book. You don't need us to tell you how to put a puzzle on a table.

INSTANT REPLAY:

at the library
the place where
ideas are grown
the books plant them
the librarians water them
until they flower and bloom
and we go and use them.

Submitted during passive program:
"write a poem about why you love the library"

2

The Gear You Need = The Gear You Have

"Why are we spending all this money on stuff?
Give 'em a pot and a wooden spoon."
—Karen Burdnell, Enoch Pratt Free Library

Passive programming is infinitely adaptable. The only limit is your imagination. You can do it inside or outside, on a wall or a table or an empty shelf—and even those minimal requirements are optional. Even if all you have is a pack of Post-It notes and a dream, you can make a passive program! Here are some ideas that will help you look at your space with new eyes and figure out what you can do with what you have.

Horizontal spaces: Tables, carts, shelves, and the Big Jar

Big table

If you've got space for a table more than two people can sit at, you're in business. One week it's covered with roll paper and provided with an inviting drawing prompt; the next, it hosts a variety of math puzzles. During your busy season, when you don't have time to change it up, cover it with a giant coloring sheet. Don't forget to position related books or other materials within sight.

Supplies for your big table:

- Roll paper
- Giant coloring sheets
- Sign holder
- Art supplies (we love stencils!)

A/V cart

Many libraries own a large, flat cart for transporting A/V or computer equipment from place to place. Chances are, that cart is only occasionally used nowadays. Turn it into an art cart, a mobile sensory exploration unit, a LEGO cart, or a game cart—because it's on wheels, you can bring it to story time to engage older children while younger siblings are singing about spiders and buses, or park it in the back of a room where an adult program is taking place so that the kids have something to do. A school group or day care shows up unexpectedly, and you don't have activities planned, or a large group of teens are hanging out after school, waiting for volleyball practice to begin? Wheel out the cart.

Decorate it with contact paper or stickers, apply fake flowers, gems, or yarn-bomb it—even better, put out the supplies and let decorating the cart become its own passive program!

All you need is a large plastic bin, so that you can easily clear off the cart and stash all your supplies in one place when someone needs the cart to transport heavy items.

Small table, book cart, counter space, or shelf

Keep your art cart looking neat.

Passive programming is a habit you are cultivating among your customers. Because it isn't directed by library staff, it should be visually appealing and in plain sight—at eye level and near the entrance to your area. This is especially important if you only have a tiny space to host it. It's also best if it's always in the same place, so that customers can get used to looking toward the same spot for your diverting and thought-provoking passive programs. At Andria's library, teens have learned to check the YA desk for worksheets and other activities as soon as they enter the teen space.

A small table, book cart, or even a spare shelf or corner of your desk can hold a Big Jar (see below) or offer activity pages and art supplies. Capture attention with:

- Tablecloth, wrapping paper, or contact paper
- Sign holder
- Literature stand
- Magnets in two colors (for voting programs)

Big Jar

Great for libraries where real estate is tight, a fishbowl, cookie jar, or one of those giant plastic jugs that cheese doodles come in can be used to collect contest entries or ballots, or to offer trivia questions, book recommendations, and more. Use it for estimation contests and the popular guessing game Books in Bits. Decorate the outside with markers, a label, or decoupage and use it over and over again.

Your Big Jar will be happiest accompanied by:

- Signage inviting participation
- Box of golf pencils

Two Big Jars and a supply of slips are all you need for an estimation contest.

Vertical spaces: Boards and walls

Whether you call it an Idea Wall, Collaboration Station, or Community Corner, it's great to have a space for self-expression. New materials like dry erase paint, magnetic primer, and chalkboard paint make it relatively easy to transform an ordinary wall into an interactive vertical space. Check the Resources Appendix for brand names and sources.

Whiteboard

On an easel or on a wall, a whiteboard is a flexible medium for polls, writing or drawing prompts, identity memes (e.g., what's your pirate name), and more. It's colorful and easily changed, and if someone writes a bad word on it, you can wipe that out without having to redo the whole thing. Plus, you can use it to announce upcoming programs and direct customers to activities. Whiteboard paint is pricey, but an easy way to turn virtually anything into a whiteboard.

You'll need:

- Whiteboard markers—the kind with an attached magnet won't walk away
- Whiteboard eraser
- Magnetic clips such as novelty magnets or old-fashioned bulldog clips
- Washi tape—your friend for marking straight lines
- Hand sanitizer (the best whiteboard cleaner we've found—it even erases marks made by permanent markers)

Chalkboard

Maybe the only wall space you have is cinderblock, and you can't get a whiteboard installed on it. Maybe it's outside, and a bulletin board would get destroyed in the weather. You can still turn it into a passive programming space. Cover it in chalkboard paint and use it the same way you'd use a whiteboard.

Customers will get a thrill out of writing on the wall, and you can use your periodic Paint Over the Wall sessions (chalkboard paint doesn't last forever) as fun community activities, too.

Pro tip: if you plan on using chalk markers on your wall, you'll want to take the extra step of putting a coat of sealant over the chalkboard paint. The chalkboard wall is a highlight of the teen space in Andria's library, but we learned the hard way that it is impossible to remove all traces of chalk marker unless you seal the wall first.

As long as you're painting the wall, you might try using a magnetic primer under the chalkboard paint. This paint is rather lightly magnetic, so two or even three coats may be necessary before it will be strong enough to hold magnetic poetry. Still, adding that functionality to your chalkboard wall opens it up to a variety of passive programming uses.

Teen lounge chalkboard.

If painting isn't an option, try magnetic chalkboard contact paper. Like the magnetic primer, this paper isn't tremendously magnetic, but it will work for alphabet magnets and magnetic poetry, and chalk takes to it just fine.

What will you need?

- Chalkboard paint
- Chalk—big chunky sidewalk chalk lasts longer and less likely to get broken
- Chalk markers
- Sponge or rag for erasing
- Soda pop—wipe your board down with a carbonated beverage to get it super clean, then wipe with water so it doesn't get sticky
- Rollers and brushes
- Dropcloth
- Optional—magnetic primer (Rust-Oleum makes the one that Paula's contractor recommended)
- Optional—clear acrylic sealant (Krylon® makes the one that Andria's team used)
- Optional—magnetic chalkboard contact paper

Wall, pillar, or post

Maybe getting your wall or post painted is just not going to happen any time soon. You can still turn it into a passive programming space using roll paper, tape, and ingenuity! Cut roll paper to fit the vertical space you have available. Tape the paper to the wall, pillar, or post. Define the area using bulletin board borders or washi tape for a more intentional look.

You can use this space for writing or drawing prompts, for a height chart, polls, or for general self-expression. You'll rip down the roll paper and start over every time your theme changes, so you might want to invest in a large roll of fairly cheap paper.

Supplies:

- Roll paper
- Bulletin board borders
- Post-Its
- Markers
- Washi tape
- Dot stickers

Easel and flip pad

Passive programming when and where you need it! Bring an easel and flip pad to your outreach events and library programs to encourage additional interaction and feedback. Great for writing prompts, drawing prompts, and especially great for polls—as every page is single use, your customers can vote with a sticker.

Supplies:

- Easel
- Flip pad—the Post-It version allows results to be displayed anywhere
- Markers
- Dot stickers

Bulletin board

The Pinterest favorite! You may already have a bulletin board, and although they're great for announcing programs and heralding the arrival of spring, why not use your bulletin board as an opportunity for interaction, not just decoration? Make the spaces you have serve as many functions as possible.

Support your interactive bulletin board with these materials:

- Tacks
- Yarn or string
- Bulldog or binder clips
- Stencils
- Post-Its
- Washi tape
- Dot stickers
- Roll paper
- Construction paper

Window or glass partition

Maybe all your vertical space is taken up by shelving. It happens. Books just line up so nicely against walls! Survey your building for a floor-to-ceiling window, glass study room wall, vestibule partition, or even a glass door that doesn't get much use.

Windows are gorgeous opportunities for passive programming that announces the vitality of your library to everyone who passes by—on either side. Make a graffiti window, a coloring window, or use washi tape to partition off comic book panels or stained-glass sections. When the sun shines, the drawings and writing will glow!

Supplies to make your window art a success include:

- Washable window markers (Crayola makes good ones)
- Liquid chalk markers (Chalkastic are widely regarded to be the best)
- Window crayons
- Washi tape or painter's tape
- Semipermanent window paint markers
- Transparency film
- Velcro dots
- Art tissue
- Post-Its

The front of your desk

The vertical space of last resort, the front of your desk can be pressed into duty as a makeshift bulletin board. You may not be able to tack things to it, but you can use tape or Post-Its to let customers (especially kid customers) respond to writing or drawing prompts or exercise their right to vote. What's the best Jolly Rancher flavor? (Answer: watermelon, obviously).

Try using contact paper to mark out a space for self-expression or to spotlight program achievements—it's exactly the right place to celebrate readers who have completed reading challenges. The magnetic chalkboard contact paper mentioned above might be just the thing for this sometimes-awkward space. Stock it with alphabet and number magnets so that toddlers have something to do while their parent or caregiver talks to library staff.

Any use of your desk for passive program space makes the service point (and you) appear more inviting, and can reduce the intimidation factor, enticing shy customers to approach. Materials to keep on hand include the following:

- Post-Its
- Sticker dots

- Scotch tape
- Washi tape or painter's tape
- Paper slips
- Roll paper
- Contact paper

Look up! Mobiles, garlands, and paper chains

Mobiles

If floor space is at a premium, try looking up! Hang a tree branch or a hula hoop from the ceiling or an exposed pipe (check with facilities staff first). Provide construction paper shapes and markers for library customers to write or draw their answers to prompts and hang them from the mobile. If the ceiling won't work, a tree branch stuck in a bucket of sand works the same way. The following are some materials you can use:

- String or yarn
- Tree branch, hula hoop, or other framework
- Clips or clothespins
- Construction paper

Garlands

Low ceilings? String a garland across a window or wall. This makes space for customers to display their responses to writing and drawing prompts, or can be used for a Clothesline Project (more on these types of projects in our chapter on Templates). Super easy to change out, a garland has a large but controlled visual impact.

Depending on your wall or window surfaces, hanging your garland may be the most challenging aspect. We've successfully used museum putty, double-sided foam tape (hard to get off most surfaces), Command strips (best for a heavier garland), glue dots (excellent for a very light garland), clear shipping tape (only thing that seems to hold up long paper chains), and more. Try these, or, if you have a very good relationship with your facilities staff, see if you can get permanent hooks installed.

Your box of garland supplies will include:

- String or yarn
- Clips or clothespins
- Hooks or adhesive for hanging

Paper chains

The humble paper chain is a surprisingly versatile and attractive display option and one that can be pressed into duty as a medium for book recommendations, voting, and even short writing prompts. Cut construction paper strips in a riot of colors—or use a themed color scheme. Put out dabbers, rubber stamps, glitter glue, paper punches in a variety of shapes, and markers for a craft table activity that helps decorate your library space.

Paper chains add dimension and color to this inventive use of vertical space.

You can use glue sticks or white school glue to put the chain links together, but the fastest glue we've found when you're connecting 100 links contributed by a preschool class—and you only have a half an hour—is Tacky Glue.

Clear shipping tape works best for hanging paper chains. You may arrange them picturesquely on top of a shelving unit or drape them around your department's sign, but do yourself a favor and tack your arrangement down with shipping tape in a couple of strategic places. Once a paper chain begins to fall, it creates a cascade that will take many nearby objects down with it. Supplies such as the following are easy to find:

- Construction paper
- Paper cutter (do yourself a favor and use a paper cutter instead of scissors!)
- Dabbers
- Rubber stamps and ink pads
- Glitter glue
- Paper punches
- Adhesive gems, tiny pompoms, googly eyes, etc.
- Markers or crayons
- Tacky Glue

Monitor

Whether it's on a cart or wall mounted, you can use a monitor for more than just games. Andria's regionally famous Best of the Web (find it in our chapter on Ideas for Any Time) is but one excellent use of a library monitor. You'll also need a computer and a cable or wireless connection.

In a perfect world, we'd all have a monitor hanging on the wall wherever we have a bunch of public computers. Sure, we'll use it to direct people to the computer that they've been assigned when their number comes up in the queue, but in a *perfect* world, that monitor would play periodic dance breaks. "Look up from your computers, folks! Take a minute to stretch and shimmy! Movement and exercise improves your mood and shakes up your brain!"

Paper

Tons of passive programming ideas need nothing more than a sheet of regular old paper. Print up puzzles, quizzes, or poetry prompts—on brightly colored paper if possible—and put them in a literature stand. Or lay them out on a table or shelf, hang them from a clip, pass them out at outreach programs, heck, toss 'em out of a plane—there is no library so small that it can't implement paper-based passive programming. You'll also need a printer and pencils.

Natural materials

Don't overlook the free resources available in your environment.

Rocks

Look for smooth stones no bigger than a fist for painting programs.

Autumn leaves

If you live in a place where trees drop their leaves in the fall, find a nice dry day to do a pickup run. Leaves make lovely additions to a mobile or garland. You can write on them, paint them, or use a hole punch to create biodegradable confetti.

Sticks or branches

A dry branch makes a lovely base for a mobile. Wedge it into a bucket of sand or hang it from the ceiling and tie or clip poems, book recommendations, or other visitor contributions.

Pine cones

Likewise, dry pine cones are easily pressed into duty as additions to a mobile or garland. Their nooks and crannies make them great for Take a Fact, Leave a Fact and other programs involving slips of paper.

Sticks in a jar—low-budget and perfectly appropriate for a Poetry Month passive program.

More multipurpose materials that you can squeak into your budget

Plastic eggs

Cheap, colorful, and easy to use over and over again, plastic eggs are a good investment, and hiding them around the library takes up no additional space. Look for big bags of these at dollar stores—and deeply discounted just after Easter.

Oversized egg timer

We use this for any type of timed challenge—quizzes, puzzles, and the physical tasks (do your favorite dance) on an Energy Circuit.

Oversized dice

Dice are great for naming memes and anything else that requires a random choice. A large foam die is less likely to get lost the first time it rolls off the table.

Shelf talkers

Homemade or professionally produced, reusable signs that dangle from shelves are great for scavenger hunts and have the added benefit of pulling customers into the stacks.

Button maker

Now, there are admittedly a lot of self-service craft tools that lend themselves to a variety of occasions, but for our money, we've never found another tool as durable, popular, versatile, and easy-to-use as a pinback button-making machine. It's a great means of self-expression, it helps you use up discarded magazines, it travels to outreach programs, and the supplies aren't that expensive.

Not to mention: "Hey, where'd you get that cool pin?" "I made it myself at the library!" Priceless.

Tote bags

Paula's library has a stash of bags dedicated to Trash or Treat (see our chapter on "The Outside World"). You can doubtless find lots of uses for these ubiquitous bookish giveaways that are currently taking up space in your closet.

Discarded library materials

Items that have been weeded from your collection for age or condition present an endless source of free passive programming supplies. Discarded magazines can be cut up for collages and button making, pages from old books can be used for blackout poetry or crafting, damaged DVDs can be decorated and hung from a mobile. Let staff know that you're interested in having a look at anything that is headed for the trash or recycling bin, and before too long, you'll be inundated with potentially useful stuff.

Almost any materials you own can lend themselves to passive programming, and we'll have lots of examples throughout this book. We've singled out the above elements—tables, carts, walls, and boards—as features that can be used and reused for a variety of programs.

INSTANT REPLAY:

The September
chalkboard prompt was:
"what are you excited to
do this school year?"

We were really upset by
one of the responses
until we realized it said
"I'm excited to do some
MATH"
- not meth.

3

Bring Your A Game:
Best Practices

Keep the customer front and center

Your first thought when designing passive programming should be: "Who am I *not* speaking to?" Identify the customers who don't attend programs or otherwise interact with staff, and figure out what appeals to those people as you move forward.

If you don't know what interests them, you can create a survey or poll to find out and use the data gathered from that passive program to create more activities.

Be mindful of the accessibility of your passive programs to non-English speakers or to people with mobility limitations or limited literacy.

Keep your programming front and center

By definition, passive programs should not rely on staff guiding people to them. When possible, put your cart, shelf, board, or table where it will be immediately seen by library customers. And keep it there—it takes longer than you think for people to remember a location.

The lobby is a key place for passive programs: customers often will notice them on their way in and participate on their way out. Also consider the places in your building where people commonly congregate. At Andria's library, a group of middle school students sit at the same table every day after school. Simply putting extra passive programming materials next to this table resulted in a marked increase in participation.

Passive programming can change as often as the weather.

Keep it fresh

Nothing's sadder than a faded bulletin board. We want our customers to develop a habit of checking to see what's new, so change up your passive programs frequently. Even if you have a weekly program like Tuesday Newsday, print it on a different color of paper every week, or use different colors within the document.

Passive programming has the advantage of being nimble. If news happens, if the weather changes, if nobody seems interested in your Match the Seed to the Full-Grown Plant game, switch it out! There's no shame in abandoning an idea that doesn't work for your customers. And even if an idea catches like wildfire and draws a lot of participation, it should be replaced before it grows stale.

It might seem intimidating to imagine coming up with a new passive programming idea every week or so, but we've found that once you develop your passive programming skills, ideas begin to multiply. This book contains tons of ideas (at least 101), but it's likely you'll outgrow our lists sooner rather than later. The good news is: by that time, you'll have the hang of it and won't need us anymore.

Keep it monitored

Even if your interactive station is out of sight of staff, make sure and swing by a few times a day. Replace depleted supplies, refresh associated book displays, keep it neat, check for inappropriate contributions to boards and murals (and try not to freak out when someone has added a bad word or anatomical cartoon—just cover it up or erase it and move on), and start conversations when you see people interacting with it. Remember: passive programming is a starting point—take advantage of these opportunities to connect with your customers and start building relationships.

Keep it visually clean and appealing

There's a fine line between fun and funky and haphazard and junky. Stay on the good side and avoid being accused of cluttering up your area by adhering to a few basic design tenets.

No handwritten signs

Unless you are an accomplished calligrapher, type up your signs and print them out. They will be easier to read and look less like those "I BUY HOUSES" signs you see tacked to telephone poles at the side of the road.

¡Usa las plantillas para contribuir a nuestro Spacescape!!

Printed signs not only look more professional, but they are easier to read—in any language.

Keep to a consistent color scheme and font for each program

All the materials and signage associated with a particular program should look similar. This is especially important with passive programs, as customers will be following visual cues without intervention or guidance from staff.

Tend your surfaces

If you are using a book cart, small table, A/V cart, or spare shelf, line your surfaces with colored or patterned contact paper or wrapping paper. Even if you yarn-bomb your cart, providing a background that is a different color than the rest of your powder-coated, putty-colored carts signals that *this* book cart (or shelf or table, etc.) is special, and you should look over here! In addition, it creates a neat, professional appearance.

Change the paper periodically to fit the theme and to stay fresh.

Pick up

For heaven's sake, don't walk by your craft table or window mural without picking up scattered crayons and putting them back in their cup. Emphasize to staff that tidying up paper scraps and putting the caps back on markers *is* in fact part of their job.

Keep staff informed and involved

Passive programming isn't just for customers. Take advantage of staff meetings, your library's Slack channel, or e-mail to keep staff abreast of your passive programming initiatives. Passive programming loses all the precious ground you've gained if the customer is coaxed into interacting with staff only to get a blank look in return.

A quick e-mail when you start an interactive passive program, telling everyone that if a kid comes up to them and tells them a joke, they're going to expect a sticker, can forestall that. Announce at the monthly staff meeting that the whiteboard wants to know everyone's favorite book series. Encourage staff to contribute to writing, drawing, and recommendation prompts—customers are more likely to participate if they see that others have, so urge staff to get the ball rolling. Prime the pump yourself by being the first to add something to the board, mobile, or garland.

Your enthusiasm will rub off and inspire other staff to find ways to engage with their customers, too. Passive programming is nothing if not fun—and fun is funner when it's shared.

Keep your materials from walking away

The first objection you might hear when you suggest introducing an unstaffed interactive element in your library is, "We'll lose all our whiteboard markers/ plastic eggs/yarn." Our automatic response to that tends to be, "How about if we address that when and if it happens?" If we try to prepare for all of the worst things that could happen, we'll never do anything!

That response doesn't always go over well, so it's also useful to have a more quantified answer in your pocket. What *if* we lose all our whiteboard markers? How much would it cost to replace them? Is there room in the department or programming budget to buy a new set?

Have you ever put out a batch of coloring sheets only to have the whole stack disappear a few hours later? It's frustrating, but what's the actual cost? A dozen sheets of copier paper and the three minutes it takes to reprint them. Passive programming is generally so low cost that these expenses can be absorbed without much effect on the bottom line.

But it's also a pain to have to track down your materials if they wander all over the library, or right out the door. Put your scissors on a string and attach it to the bulletin board. Glue a magnet or attach Velcro to the markers so that they can be replaced on the frame or windowsill. Craft table supplies should live in pencil cups, caddies, trays, or baskets, not scattered on the table.

Give customers a dedicated place for supplies, and they'll be much less likely to absent-mindedly stuff them in their pocket.

Make the rules crystal clear

If it's a contest, decide on a deadline, judging period, and a date for announcing the winners. Will you allow multiple entries? Make that clear on the contest materials. If you've got a scavenger hunt going on, note the time limit on the game sheet. How many questions do they have to get right on their trivia quiz in order to win a prize? How many times can they guess if they get it wrong?

Rules are especially important as we communicate with other staff and of course should be applied consistently.

Ideally, we'd decide all of our rules at the outset—but every time we've tried a new type of passive program, a new rule has announced itself once we're a little ways in. Egg hunts are great for sending small customers into the furthest nooks and crannies of the library. But how many eggs do they need to find in order to get a prize? And what's the limit? Less than 24 hours into Paula's first hunt, her staff realized "Re-hide the egg, and *then* come back for your prize," was an essential rule. This is called being flexible and responsive and is nothing to apologize for.

Provide additional information

In the olden days, we regarded programming as bait to get people into the library so that we could coax 'em into checking out books. Now we regard good programming as a goal in and of itself—but that doesn't mean we'll turn our noses up at an additional circ or two.

When your passive program catches the eye of an interested customer, make sure you are also pointing that person at further resources. Especially since passive programming tends to engage people who may be reluctant to approach a staff member with questions, this is an opportunity not to be wasted. Take advantage of the curiosity your activity sparks—it's a chance to increase circulation, highlight what the library has to offer, and, best of all, anticipate the needs and interests of your customers.

If you put out a word search or a maze, add the call number information for where customers can find puzzle books. Set up a display of comics next to the drawing table where customers are encouraged to design their own superhero costume. Put how-to-draw books on your Art Cart.

You get the idea, but here are some more examples:

Skills signpost

Keep a sign holder on the craft table. Use it to let parents know what skills their children are practicing when they draw with stencils or make a pinback button.

Post a flyer on the benefits of early literacy featuring well-known children's book characters next to a Draw Your Favorite Character challenge.

If you have a central location for flyers and calendars, devote a section to information relevant to whatever passive program you have going on right now, whether it's current events literacy, vocabulary building, numeracy, or the like.

Materials map

Use your sign holder to display directions to the graphic novel section (you might literally draw a map if no library map is available and if your orthographic skills are up to it) when you have blank comic sheets available for Adventures of My Pet or What's Your Manga Identity. If you're fortunate enough to have a bird-watching window, display books about birds available for checkout—and tag the birdfeeder with the call number that will take them to bird identification guides.

Community resource list

Make bookmarks listing relevant community resources and set them out next to your activity. Customers who complete your Seed Match Game might get a bookmark listing the farmers markets in your area. Trash or Treat litter picker-uppers get a bookmark with information on bulk trash pickup, household hazardous waste drop-off sites and times, and more. Place voter registration forms next to a whiteboard poll to "Vote for the best cheese" or "Nominate a fictional character for president."

Craft instruction takeaway

Provide instructions for duplicating a craft at home. Make copies and put these in a literature stand.

Booklist

There's nothing wrong with an old-fashioned booklist. Whip one up (or steal from online or one of the upcoming chapters in this book) and post copies as part of your interactive displays.

Program flyers

And for Pete's sake, have copies of your monthly program schedule close at hand at all times.

Collect contact information

Passive programs can come in handy for future marketing purposes. Make it a habit to ask for e-mail addresses on contest entry forms. Add these to any e-mail lists you use to promote library programs.

Try to incorporate a recursive element

Passive programming is a great way to get customers to engage with the library space even if they're reluctant to talk to library staff. But the cleverest passive programming incorporates at least one brief staff transaction. This creates an opening to establish trust and a relaxed relationship.

As librarians, it's often hard for us to remember that not everyone expects us to be friendly or helpful. We have to sneak up on 'em sometimes. A recursive element that requires the customer to have a second interaction (to claim their prize, or submit their entry form) gives you an opportunity to reinforce the message that you are, in fact, neither judgmental nor intimidating and strengthen that newly formed bond.

Tell me a joke (fact, poem, etc.)

Passive programs that challenge the customer to find something in the library and tell it to a staff member for a prize are an ideal conversation starter. Jokes, poems, facts—be ready with your own joke/poem/fact in return, and you're off and running.

This is a wonderful way to use those plastic eggs we mentioned in the chapter on materials. Call them dinosaur, dragon, or bird eggs, and you can use them any time of year. Print jokes or fun facts—and instructions to share the contents with a staff member—on slips of paper, fold them up, and stuff them in the eggs, and then hide the eggs in the stacks. Young people will likely open an egg if they stumble across one—it's their nature—but grownups may need a bit more encouragement. You may want to write, "If you find me, open me!" on the eggs or post signage inviting customers to actively hunt for them.

Enter to win

This is the easiest recursive passive program of them all—reel 'em back in to find out if they've won or to collect their prize. We've had customers guess/estimate the number of jelly beans in a jar, how many books are taken out of the library in a week, how many milk jugs were used to make the Milk Jug Igloo. We've named mascots and trees, collected secrets, poems, and votes. Many, or even most, passive programs can be adapted to the Enter to Win modality. Be wary about giving a prize to "the best" entry, as that is subjective and can result in hurt feelings. Either have an objectively correct answer, or select winners randomly.

Book recommendations

A great example of a passive program that can turn into an active staff interaction is the peer book recommendation. Library staff are used to recommending books—it's a big part of what we do. But we do not always present as well-credentialed experts: a 53-year-old white lady may in fact know her hard sci-fi from Asimov to Zelazny, but she may not fit the reader's preconception of what a stone-cold supergeek looks like.

Passive programming can help, providing the reader with book ideas and eventually giving library staff a chance to prove their worth.

Collect peer recommendations

What's the last book you read that made you laugh out loud? What's the scariest book you ever read? Share a great book for a rainy day—there are endless prompts for book suggestions. If you do this on a whiteboard or a bulletin board, recommendations are instantaneous. No wall space? Make a slip that a customer can fill out and drop in a jar. Most importantly, collect all the recommended titles and turn them into visible results: a handout booklist, a display, or both.

Create an anonymous source

He craves realistic romance novels but would be mortified to ask. She wants something *really scary* but doesn't want the old lady behind the desk to think she's a psycho by asking for serial killer fiction. (Fun fact: lots of old lady librarians read a ton of super scary stuff!)

Booklists and displays are fine solutions to this problem, but you can up your game with a fun, interactive passive program like a Genre Jar or What Should I Read Next flowchart. Look for these in our chapter on Ideas for Any Time.

These types of passive programs enable customers to view the library as more than just a book depository but as a trusted source for recommendations. When a customer sees their contribution valued and shared, they are no longer a visitor but a resource, a community member, even an expert. All of this can make them feel more confident about using the library, less intimidated by librarians, and more likely to approach staff for recommendations in the future.

Blind Date with a Book

Blind Date with a Book is a display idea that enjoys a brief vogue from time to time. Librarians like it because it makes for an eye-catching visual; we support the idea of people breaking out of their reading ruts, and the book-as-love-interest concept tickles us. We also think it's cool that the books can be checked out without being unwrapped (either through RFID or by photocopying the bar code and sticking it on the back). Yeah, we're all nerds.

The element of surprise appeals to customers and the books disappear from the display, but it's hard to gauge whether people actually like the mystery book they took home, and as you know, a display by itself is not a passive program, no matter how much time you spend decorating the wrapped books with heart-shaped stickers.

So, how do you make the most of the time you spent wrapping books and turn this display into a passive program that can be quantified and has a recursive element? Add a Rate Your Date slip that can be returned to the desk to be entered for a prize. This idea incorporates Book Recommendations with Enter to Win—a double dip!

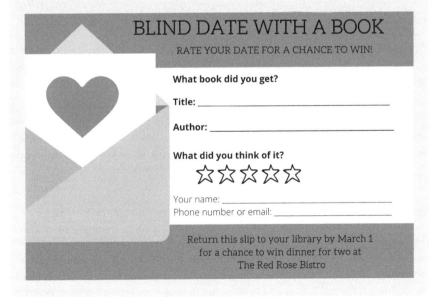

BLIND DATE WITH A BOOK

RATE YOUR DATE FOR A CHANCE TO WIN!

What book did you get?

Title: _____

Author: _____

What did you think of it?

☆ ☆ ☆ ☆ ☆

Your name: _____
Phone number or email: _____

Return this slip to your library by March 1
for a chance to win dinner for two at
The Red Rose Bistro

Reward participation

Contests, quizzes, scavenger hunts, word puzzles, cleanup—all can be rewarded with a prize. You put away the blocks in the baby area? Come to the desk to get a prize. Finished the trivia quiz? Show it to library staff and they'll give you a prize—even if you didn't get all the questions right. Now you have an opportunity to initiate a conversation. "You cleaned up? Let's go look! Wow, you did a great job! Thank you!" Look over their solution to the puzzle, give them their prize, and then walk them over to where puzzle books are shelved.

For a lot of people, especially young kids, the prize becomes secondary after a while. Positive attention from a grownup can be its own reward. When they turn in that worksheet, turn on the praise: "Good job! I'm proud of you!"

Candy is dandy

If your library system allows you to give out candy, go for it. Don't buy candy with nuts, and chocolate generally has a shorter shelf life than Jolly Ranchers, Starbursts, Smarties, or Skittles. Point out where they can put their trash. "Thank you in advance for putting your candy wrapper in that garbage can!" If a parent is present, check with them before handing candy to their child. Always have a backup in case the parent puts the kibosh on the sweet stuff.

Pro tip: No Nerds, unless you really enjoy tweezing up tiny pieces of crushed candy from the carpet.

Stickers are quicker

Make a fancy box for individual stickers (cut up sticker sheets or strips if necessary) and let kid customers pick from a variety when they perform a sticker-worthy service or hand in an activity sheet. Temporary tattoos work too.

Vinyl stickers for laptops and water bottles are popular with teens and tweens and are a cost-effective alternative to candy. The lid of your sticker box is a handy spot for keeping a Post-It on which you can record a running tally of how many stickers you give out—good for stats!

Our contribution to global warming

We are as antiplastic as anyone, but you'll find us trawling the Oriental Trading website in a heartbeat when our leftover summer reading prizes run out. Spider rings, monster finger puppets, novelty erasers, plastic kazoos—chances are you've been down this road before and know what to look for. Here are a few reminders:

- Avoid toys with violent or excessively vulgar themes.
- Be mindful of choking hazards.
- Remember your budget.
- Watch quantities in the item description. Have you ever ordered what you thought was a gross of fancy pencils only to open the box to find a dozen? That's a real fling-your-reading-glasses-across-the-room moment!
- Bouncy balls are tiny pellets of evil mayhem and should be shunned.

Give a book

Don't let new nonlibrary copies of books linger in your closet. ARCs and summer reading prizes rarely age well. Give them out as prizes whenever you can—and when possible, allow customers to pick from a selection: a free book that doesn't fit someone's interests is little better than a doorstop.

Dedicate a book

Here's a big reward for a big accomplishment. We first heard about this from Cindy Ritter and Ginny Reese of Jefferson-Madison Regional Library, where it's used as a reward for completing their 1,000 Books Before Kindergarten family reading goal—but it is doubtless used at libraries around the country.

At JMRL, when parents present their completed reading log, their child gets to pick their favorite book in the collection. Let's say three-year-old Amina's favorite book is *Hungry Jim* by Laurel Snyder. A bookplate is added to that book's inside front cover with Amina's name, age, and the date. Now Amina has a permanent place in her library—and is she likely to run to the shelves to visit "her" book every time she's in the library? Of course she is.

In addition, the next person to pick this book up sees that it comes highly recommended by an expert, validating this book about a boy and his unusual breakfast as an exceptional choice. There you go. One guaranteed checkout circ.

INSTANT REPLAY:

A boy tried, unsuccessfully, to Google the answer to his Black History Trivia question

Me: "Listen up friend, I'm going to lay a little truth on you. Sometimes the answers you seek are not on the internet but...wait for it...IN A BOOK. Like maybe this one! Let's look in this thing called the index. Look for Nobel Prize. What page does that say? Cool, go read that page and come back with an answer."

5 minutes later...

Him: "It's Toni Morrison!"

Me:: "YESSSSSSSS! YOU DID IT! AND YOU USED A BOOK! Here, you can have two pieces of candy. Now go tell all your friends that books are awesome.".

4

Covering All the Bases: Passive Program Templates

Although there are definitely passive programs that are screamingly unique and unlike anything you've ever seen before, many if not most are variations on a few basic types. Once you figure out a great way to present, for example, What's Your Manga Name? at your library, you can adapt that naming meme format to a variety of occasions. Cowboy, Pirate, Ninja, Alien, Fantasy Warrior, Clown, Roller Derby, Drag Queen/King—easy, once you know how!

So, rather than repeating similar instructions for every one of the fabulous writing prompts, polls, and other activities mentioned in this book, this chapter provides templates for some of the main types of passive programming that we've used successfully at our libraries over the years. We'll show you how to implement them using the various resources we listed in our chapter on materials—tables, boards, carts, hanging displays, and the Big Jar.

Try as we might, we haven't been able to make every type of passive programming work with every passive programming modality. But don't take our word for it—we thought you couldn't do a passport program on a post until Meredith Veatch at Enoch Pratt Free Library in Baltimore said, "Make name tags and move them up the post every time they hit a milestone." Genius!

Experiment, adapt, and tweak your programming until it fits your unique needs, space, and resources.

Prompts

Professional conferences and book festivals frequently use writing prompts to gather opinions and provoke reflection—it can be a great way to take the temperature of your attendees. But these Post-It walls or giant whiteboards also serve as icebreakers. Strangers meet when they swap Sharpies or comment

Passive programming can have an unexpectedly arresting visual impact.

on previous posts. Shy people are provided something to talk about. What a great way to gently encourage socialization and help people feel like they belong.

Grease the wheels of interaction and engagement at your library with a tantalizing question or concept to inspire answers and artwork. You'll find dozens of examples in upcoming chapters, and in this section, you'll learn how to set them up.

Fill in the blank, recommendations, and drawing prompts

Wall or drawing table

Writing, recommendation, and drawing prompts are easy to set up on any vertical or horizontal space that can be written upon—a whiteboard, window, easel, chalkboard, or drawing table. Just write the question in large letters at the top or in the middle and leave plenty of space for responses.

Bulletin board or desk front

Post the question and provide Post-Its, paper slips, or construction paper shapes to use for responses, as well as pushpins or tape so participants can post their answers or drawings.

Big Jar

Part of what's thought-provoking about prompts is seeing how other people answered the question. You lose this aspect when you use a Big Jar, but at times that can work in your favor.

Write the question on the outside of the jar or use a sign, and provide slips and pencils for your customers to write their answers. In this case, you might want to document all the answers and put them on display—ideally, in the same place as the jar. Use a sign holder, stick the answers on a piece of poster board, or use them to decorate the jar itself.

Writing prompts that touch on more personal subjects actually benefit from the privacy of the Big Jar approach. People will respond more thoughtfully and honestly when they can answer anonymously.

- What's something you really like about yourself?
- What's your deepest fear?
- What question about yourself are you very tired of answering?

Monitor

Most people know how to use PowerPoint. Create a slideshow with your questions, and let customers add their answers on a connected laptop while the slides play continuously on the monitor. Fiddle with the laptop display settings and PowerPoint View settings so that the slideshow can be edited while playing.

This works best with writing and recommendation prompts, but the most digitally savvy librarians will figure out how to use their monitor to display responses to drawing prompts, too.

Mobile or garland

Print out your prompt and hang it centrally on your mobile or garland or place it in a sign holder next to the supplies. Set out thematically appropriate construction paper shapes—hearts, leaves, stars, pennant shapes, flags—and short lengths of yarn or mini clips. If you have a die-cut machine such as an Ellison® or a Cricut®, take full advantage of it to make fun, thematically appropriate shapes. Your mobile or garland will gradually fill up with answers to your question.

Installing the "I Have a Dream" mobile at Southeast Anchor Library in Baltimore.

Caption this

What's going on here? What could that guy be thinking? Caption contests are a kind of prompt that utilizes and develops skills in visual and verbal literacy and even social-emotional skills. You'll find lots of caption prompts in our chapter "A Year of Passive Programming"—here's how to make them work with the resources you have.

Paper

Simply insert the picture in a Word document and add blank lines below. Don't forget to put a space for the person to write their name. If you want to give a prize to the funniest or most thought-provoking caption, the paper method makes it easy to identify and reward the winner and ensures no entries are accidentally erased or removed.

Whiteboard, chalkboard, drawing table, or bulletin board

Affix the image to the board or draw one freehand, if you have that gift, and let customers write their captions or dialogue in the remaining space.

Big Jar

The Big Jar is best suited to a reverse caption contest—fill the jar with a batch of silly snippets of dialogue and provide blank panel sheets for customers to draw a corresponding scene—but you could also fill the jar with various images and have participants randomly select one to caption.

Monitor

Make a PowerPoint of intriguing pictures to run continuously on the monitor while customers add captions to the PowerPoint on a laptop.

Mobile

Print your funny photo in color and hang it prominently on the mobile. Provide paper word balloon shapes for customers to write their captions on.

Activity sheets: Quizzes, worksheets, games, and puzzles

Paper-based programs are an easy fallback, and every one of them is a skills-building exercise. Word searches foster literacy and improve spelling, and teach new vocabulary words through context. Mazes sharpen executive functioning and problem-solving skills. Quizzes develop research skills and critical thinking.

When people work together as a team to solve these puzzles and answer these questions, they gain practice with interpersonal skills and evaluating information.

These self-directed activities are excellent to have on hand for children and teens, although it's likely you'll need to provide a small incentive (everyone likes a prize!) to motivate older kids to participate. Teens will happily spend 20 minutes completing a current events quiz to get a lollipop, but if the quiz is offered only as something to alleviate boredom, odds are they won't touch it. Word searches, mazes, match games, and quizzes show up all over this book—especially in our chapter on a Week of Passive Programming.

Paper

Even if all you've got is a printer and some paper, you're set for passive programming success! Quizzes, word searches, and mazes are good for the brain and great opportunities to lavish praise on people who complete them. Set these worksheets on the corner of your desk, on tables, or wherever customers will find them.

Be sure the worksheet has clear instructions to return the paper to the desk for a prize when completed, and always put a space for the participant to write their name. Now you can greet them personally the next time they're in the library.

Use a magnetic clip to offer quizzes or pencil puzzles on a whiteboard.

Whiteboard, chalkboard, or bulletin board

Use magnetic clips or binder clips to make your puzzles and quizzes available on the board.

Big table

If you have a drawing table, offer your activity sheets on a tray or in a literature stand. Use the remaining vertical or horizontal board or table space to offer hints and directions. "Work in groups or on your own to complete the quiz! Get four answers right to win a prize!"

Big Jar

A Big Jar is an easy way to do trivia contests: just print out a numbered list of questions, cut into strips, and put them in the jar—people pull a random question and try to answer it. Your Big Jar is also a way to put a twist on freaky facts and current events challenges. Print headlines or facts on slips of paper, including a number of false items. The challenge? Figure out whether the "fact" you picked out is true or false. This is a great conversation starter.

Monitor

Do you Kahoot? Chances are the kids in your library do. Get to know this free quiz app and let it loose in your library.

Mobile or garland

Not the most optimal vector for worksheets and quizzes, but you can still use your hanging passive programming for trivia questions or a mesmerizing True or False game. Print true and false facts on cards you hang from your mobile or garland. Keep the answer key nearby!

Name generators

Challenge customers to look inside themselves and determine their alter egos. This can be free association ("What's your DJ name?") or you can provide a template. "Your monster name is the name of your first pet +birthstone + favorite food+ the word 'monster.'" Provide nametags so that Fluffy Emerald Sushi Monster can proudly announce her identity to the world.

Devise name correlation tables to make this activity a bit more challenging and guarantee hilarious results. Find them online or make your own:

- Decide on a template for the name. For example, a pirate name like Mad Jack the Stinky Seafarer has four pieces: Adjective, First Name, "the," Adjective, and Noun. (Four pieces is extremely ambitious—two will usually do.)
- Next, come up with lists of humorous adjectives, names, and nouns that fit the theme.
- Correlate those lists with personal variables: color of your socks, month you were born, siblings (brother, sister, none, both), pets, and so forth.

This may seem confusing now, but once you get the hang of it, we promise it's not hard!

Voice of experience tip: we tend to use "color of your socks" rather than shirt because so many kids come in to our libraries after school wearing their school uniforms.

You'll find loads of naming memes in upcoming chapters, and here's how to implement them:

Paper or monitor

Type up correlation tables: list "month you were born" alongside humorous cowboy names, or list "color of your socks" opposite planetary origin. Print the page or drop the lists into a PowerPoint.

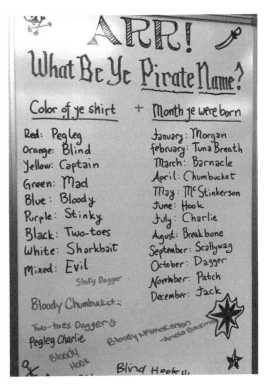

Correlation tables invite customers to discover their pirate name.

Whiteboard, bulletin board, or chalkboard wall

Write the rules of the meme and clip blank name tags to your board. If someone is One-Eyed Stinkfoot Pete for the day, we all deserve to know about it.

Big Jar

Print titles, descriptive adjectives, first names, last names, and so forth on different-colored paper. "Pick one yellow, one pink, and one green slip—put them together to find your Interstellar Alien name!" Don't forget the name tags—putting the slips in order and copying "Prince Florpal De gustibus of Saturn" onto a name tag adds a skills-building component to this silly activity.

Mobile or garland

Have participants make a second nametag to hang from your garland or mobile. Affix a sign saying "Meet our Pirates" (or Aliens, or Monsters, etc.).

Table

Choose six options for each category (title, first name, last name, etc.), print them, and slip them in a sign holder. Stand the sign holder on your table along with a big foam die (look for sources in the Appendix). Library visitors roll the die to find their manga name, cowboy name, pet name, or pirate name.

You can also try this using the folded paper fortune-telling contraption known colloquially in some regions as a "cootie catcher." It's awfully difficult to describe, so google "cootie catcher," and chances are you'll recognize it immediately.

It's easiest if you print a template for your fortune teller. Write each naming option in the correct space on the template; then follow instructions to fold it into shape.

Polls

A passive program that requires little time but sometimes lots of thought from its participants, polls can be binary (Yes/No, This or That) or multiple choice. The poll itself and the results are excellent conversation starters.

Set them up the following ways.

Bulletin board

Pose your question; then section off the answer areas with washi tape or marker lines. Provide sticker dots, pushpins, or Post-Its so that passersby can vote.

Whiteboard or chalkboard

Here's an example: "What's the best superpower?" Label one side of the board "Flying" and the other "Invisibility." Leave room at the bottom of the board for "Other." Section off the answer areas with washi tape or marker lines. Show people how to vote by adding a few hashmarks (or magnet dots if your board is magnetic) yourself.

NOTE: Don't use sticker dots on whiteboards. You *can* get that adhesive off, but it's not easy.

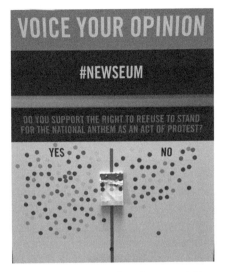

A current events poll welcomes visitors to the Newseum in Washington, DC. Polls turn visitors into participants and can give you valuable cultural insights in the bargain.

Book cart or shelf

Post the question in a sign holder. Section off spaces for the Yeas and Nays with washi tape. Provide colored magnets for voting. Or set out labeled clear jars and marbles or pompoms to drop in to cast your vote.

Monitor

Set out a laptop with a SurveyMonkey or Google poll and connect it to the screen. Periodically refresh the results and display them on your wall-mounted or cart-mounted monitor. Or use a browser-based survey program like Minti that works well on mobile devices.

Mobile or garland

Print the poll question—for instance, "Who would win in a fight?" at the top or base of your hanging installation, and provide colored pieces of paper for customers to add: gold for one contender—let's call her Katniss—and blue for her opponent, hmm . . . how about Harry Potter? Results will be visible at a glance.

Big Jar

Post the question and provide balls or paper slips in two colors for voting. A clear jar will show which "side" is winning—or use two jars side by side—but be sure to count the votes and post a tally when the voting period is over.

Big Jars work best with This or That, Yes or No, and other polls with limited or binary answers.

Scavenger hunts

An evergreen favorite—and for good reason—scavenger hunts encourage customers to scrutinize the library, discovering resources and treasures along the way. Your scavenger hunt items can include fixed features, such as the copier or the graphic novel section, flexible answers like "find a book with a red cover," or specially placed items. Salt your library with portraits of African American heroes for a Black History Month Scavenger Hunt, or park stuffed animals on low shelves and challenge kids to find them all.

Scavenger hunt lists have to be portable, so printing them on paper is the easiest option. For pre-readers, take a picture of each item and insert the pictures in a Word table. Though this template doesn't adapt well to the other modalities, it can be a means to direct patrons toward other passive programs in your library, if the scavenger hunt requires them to find the daily whiteboard poll or count the number of blue slips hanging from the mobile.

Egg hunts

What would you do if you found a brightly colored plastic egg nestled beside the shark books? You'd open it, of course! For passive programs, we prefer indoor egg hunts to outside ones. Less chance of your eggs (and customers!) getting muddy, broken, lost, wet, or buggy.

1. Stuff plastic eggs with fun facts, questions, poems, or jokes and instructions to share the contents with a library staff member for a prize.
2. Collect the eggs at the desk (don't forget to keep a tally for your stats!).
3. Take the fact or joke slip, switch it for a new one, and send the finder back out into the library to hide their egg for the next person to find—the only thing more fun than finding an egg is hiding it.

Because the instructions are inside the eggs, you don't need to create signage for this one. Let people experience the surprise of finding an unexpected "treasure" and seeing what's inside.

Although they are not required for this type of passive program, you can use your whiteboard, bulletin board, or other surfaces to post the jokes or facts as they are found. This will highlight the program and encourage other library users to search actively for eggs. You'll find more ideas for using eggs throughout this book, but we're not going to tell you where—you have to hunt for them!

Take a fact, leave a fact

A quicker and less chaotic passive program involving facts, jokes, or poems makes use of a Big Jar and user contributions. Print out a number of fun facts or clean jokes (or poems or thought prompts, etc.), cut them into slips, fold them, and add them to your jar. Provide blank slips in a box next to the jar. Print an attractive sign: "Free Jokes" is a good one, or "Get Smarter Just by Putting Your Hand in This Jar."

You can require a joke or fact contribution as payment for taking a slip, or just suggest it. This program is a great low-space option for heritage months, poetry month, or any time.

Custodianship activities

Offer prizes for picking up library toys or start a "Trash or Treat" program that rewards kids for collecting trash outside the building. Provide supplies such as reusable garbage bags and gloves for trash collection. Be sure the rules are clearly stated—don't pick up sharp things, leaves are not trash, and so forth—and don't send young children out to wander the streets unaccompanied!

Parents especially appreciate it when you reward actions like these, as they reinforce responsible behaviors, good citizenship, and environmental awareness.

With this sort of passive programming, you can use your whiteboard or other resources to acknowledge the "Good Citizens of the Week": kids can add

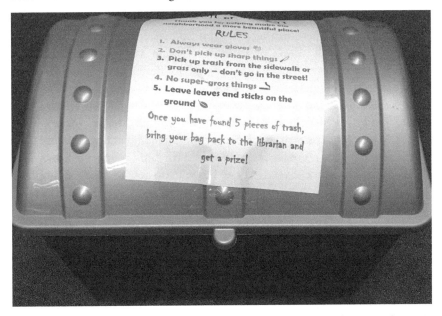

Paula's Trash or Treat treasure chest holds reusable trash bags, gloves, and MANY copies of the 5 Rules for Successful Sanitation.

their name to the board, mobile, and so on after completing the task. This will generate pride, boost awareness, and encourage additional participation.

Clothesline projects

Use twine or yarn to create a clothesline on a wall, on a bulletin board, or in a window. Set out T-shirts, handkerchiefs, lengths of wide ribbon, or fabric squares along with glitter glue or fabric markers. Customers are asked to decorate the object with a message related to a given theme and then tie or clip their creation to the line.

This kind of passive program lends itself beautifully to programs in support of community awareness of issues like violence prevention, mental health, domestic violence, and LGBTQ+ issues, or to help a community heal after tragedy. Accompany this with related books, videos, and a list of relevant websites and hotline numbers.

Passport programs

Programs that include some kind of reading or activity log are omnipresent in libraries. Participants are challenged to read a certain number or types of books or perform reading-related activities. They are responsible for filling out their own log or recording their accomplishments in an online program such as Beanstack or ReadSquared, and they get prizes at intervals and after completing the challenge.

Most of our Summer Reading programs fall into this category. Even though we don't traditionally think of Summer Reading as a passive program, it checks all the boxes: it's a self-directed activity done at one's one pace with no set schedule, it's a starting point for relationship building, and it's a tried and true way to extend library programming into the home, with return visits to the library baked right in. Other programs in this category include 1,000 Books Before Kindergarten, Book Bingo, and themed reading challenges. See chapters 7 and 9 for more ideas for Passport Programs.

We're pretty confident we don't need to tell you how to run a reading program any more than we need to tell you how to put a puzzle on a table, but there are a few best practices to keep in mind:

- Find a vertical space, mobile, or garland where you can post the names of people who completed the program.
- Keep documentation easy—use a bookmark or a punch card and don't require that participants write down titles if your program asks them to read more than about ten books.
- Support your program with activity sheets and displays that fit the theme.

These broad categories of passive programming are just a start. You may be inspired to find success with an innovative idea that's never even occurred to us (and if you do, let us know about it!)

Passive programming is fun, so have fun with it! Try something, and then try something else; combine different elements in new ways, always keeping in mind the ultimate goals of library engagement, entertainment, and challenge.

INSTANT REPLAY:

Teenager: "here, I finished my word search"

Me: [checks answer key]: "oops, you missed one"

Them: [shrugs]: "I don't care"

The word they missed was "apathy"

5

Run Up the Score and Win Fans: Stats and Sharing

If you are at all like us, you are way more excited by words, ideas, and human contact than by numbers, and you are tempted to breeze past this chapter, but STOP. This is important. Programming has replaced circulation as the gold standard by which we measure the effectiveness and reach of public libraries. The most recent Public Library Service Survey shows a 27% increase in programming per capita since 2012, compared to marked decreases in circulation, visitation, and reference interactions.

Further, this study, conducted annually by the Institute for Museum and Library Services, indicates that while public library use nationwide has increased, circulation has declined in many systems. This makes it more important than ever to record usage statistics such as program attendance to include in reports to administrators and other stakeholders. Libraries offer far more to their customers than books alone—they present a wealth of learning and enrichment opportunities to members of their communities.

Public libraries in particular are dependent on support from their community and legislators. Budgets are determined by a variety of factors at the local and national level, and the unfortunate reality is we must constantly advocate for our libraries and departments to prove our value, fight budget cuts, and request additional staff and funding. A combination of cold, hard statistics that quantify our work and heartwarming photos that illustrate it makes a powerful and difficult to ignore statement, whether you are seeking money and support from within your organization or without.

When you are attempting to build partnerships within your community or solicit donations from local businesses, your pitch should include how they will benefit from the relationship, and usage statistics are the key to demonstrating this. Help potential supporters recognize that their donation is not just feel-good philanthropy but also a powerful marketing tool that will increase public awareness of their services and products.

"We're looking for a local business to help support our after-school programming, in which 10,000 kids from this community participate annually. We would put your logo on all our promotional materials which would be seen by the kids, their parents and caregivers." A savvy business owner will appreciate the value of reaching such a wide audience at a nominal cost.

All library staff should be on their toes about programming statistics—what counts and how to record them, report them, and wield them effectively. Having stats in your pocket and at the tip of your tongue gives you swagger, and who doesn't need more of that?

Passive programming "counts"

Don't for one second think that claiming tallies and head counts from passive programming in your statistical reports is cheating. We run into this mindset often, and we are here to set you straight! The word "passive" is highly misleading and unfortunately undersells our efforts.

Not only does this kind of programming require active work on your part to prepare, promote, and maintain, but it also reaches customers and engages them on an individual level as much as—perhaps even more than—staff-led programming. When a customer picks up a trivia question and uses library resources to solve it, they are exercising their own skills rather than being led by hand. When a kid casts their vote for their favorite graphic novel character, they are making their mark on the library for all to see. When a teen uses your magnetic poetry set to express themselves, they are not just developing creativity and literacy skills, they are doing important identity work.

Every single time someone engages with a passive program you created, they are interacting with library staff and resources in some way, and that matters. They deserve to be counted. And your work in creating that opportunity deserves to be recognized.

Including these numbers in your monthly reports is a solid, quantifiable way to show administrators and Board members that your library is a vibrant and engaging environment, that you are dedicated to adding value to users' library experience, and that a budget increase and/or additional staffing is entirely justified, if not grossly needed. It also helps your overall average and gives you a solid base of numbers to report, on the off chance one of your staff-led programs that month was a flop.

You want to keep this data for your own records too. They will help you evaluate your efforts and determine which types and themes of passive programs garner the most attention and participation at your location. This information is essential when deciding how much of next year's budget to allocate for passive programming supplies and incentives. It also comes in handy when considering your department's workload and workflow.

If your system doesn't require it (and even if it does), we highly recommend maintaining a separate spreadsheet where you can track your program statistics over time. Instead of just saying, "We need more money and staff," you will be able to state with authority, "Our program participation has increased 50% since last year and we need more resources to meet our community's growing needs." You'll have the data to back it up and can provide a compelling argument for increasing your programming budget and staffing levels. And boom! There's that swagger we were talking about.

Keeping score

So, how do you quantify customer participation in self-directed activities?

It depends on the program. Since the primary goal of passive programming is engagement and interaction, you will want to find a way to track every instance of such. Here are some techniques that have worked in our libraries and others. It may take a few attempts to find the one that's most effective for your situation, but it is worth the effort.

As in active programs, a clicker is a stat counter's best friend. Staff in Paula's department wear one on a lanyard when a program is going on—a fashionable and useful accessory that serves as an ever-present reminder to click those stats.

Some of these methods involve staff observing and counting customers who interact with passive programs independently. This requires that library workers monitor their areas closely, which has the added benefits of increasing opportunities for interacting with customers and helping to keep the library a safe place for all users.

However, don't overwhelm your coworkers who will be tracking participation—give them plenty of notice, simple instructions, and a centrally located tally sheet, and don't have more of these programs going on at once than the frontline staff can reasonably manage.

Activity sheets and contests

Count the activity sheets or quizzes turned in for a prize. A convenient way to do this is to make an answer key (just do the quiz yourself and get all the answers right—don't bother typing up a separate sheet) and park it on a clipboard. Make a hashmark on a corner of this page for every sheet you "grade."

To make an activity sheet program truly passive, post the answer sheet in a central location, along with a tray for completed sheets. Customers can check their answers themselves, and at closing you collect and count the sheets from the bin. (If you do this, you are missing out on the chance to interact personally with your participants, but if your staffing situation is dire, this may be the way to go.)

At Andria's library, teens who complete word searches and other activity sheets can turn in one per day for a piece of candy. Because it is a teenager's job to push boundaries and seek ways to circumvent the rules, they will occasionally try to get additional pieces of candy by turning in a new worksheet with each shift change. For this reason, we insist the teens write their name on their work, and we keep all the sheets collected that day at the desk, so we know who has already participated. At the end of the day, we count the sheets and add the number to our daily usage statistics.

Try turning your whiteboard or chalkboard into a Wall of Fame for Tuesday Newsday or other contests. Enhance your gaming area with a board that lets gamers document their name (or game alias) and high score. Participants get bragging rights, and you get stats: everybody wins!

Find a fact, stump the librarian, trivia, jokes, and others

Keep a numbered sheet at the service desk and ask people to write their names when they correctly answer a trivia question or find a fact. At the end of the program, you don't even have to count the names.

Alternatively, keep a tally slip on the sticker or candy box and ask staff to make a mark every time they give out a prize. Start a new count every reporting period. Consider keeping track of wrong answers and aborted attempts as well.

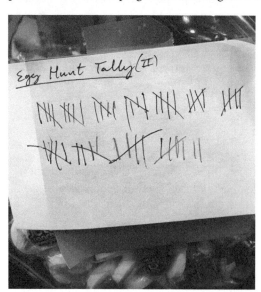

Stats tallies don't have to be pretty to get the job done!

This will give you insight into whether your challenges are on par with your customers' abilities, and it lets every attempt and interaction count toward your total.

You can also keep a tally sheet at the desk and mark it every time a customer approaches and reads a poem, tells a joke or a fun fact, or says "Hello, my name is _____" in sign language. Level up: if a customer approaches a service desk and reads a poem in sign language, give them all the candy, claim seven passive programming interactions, and call it a day!

Writing and drawing prompts

Count the answers given to the writing or drawing prompt. Yes, this means standing in front of the whiteboard/chalkboard/bulletin board and counting with your finger. If you feel silly doing this, take a picture with your phone and do the counting at your desk when you are writing your monthly report or filling out the stats spreadsheet.

Voting for favorites

Just like in real elections, every vote counts! At the end of the voting period, count the ballots in the box, the sticker dots on the poll, the hash marks on the whiteboard, or the responses clipped to the mobile.

Big Jar programs

If customers are taking slips of paper with book recommendations or trivia questions from the jar, count the number of slips you load into the Big Jar to start—then count the number left at the end of the program and subtract.

If your Big Jar functions as a collection point for guesses, votes, or other contributions, count the number of items in the jar every day, week, or at the end of the program.

If your Big Jar is used for a "guess how many" game, count the number of guesses you receive.

Egg hunts

Did you fill a bunch of plastic eggs and hide them throughout the library? Collect the plastic eggs as they are turned in and count them at the end. Did you just hide one egg that the finder is tasked with re-hiding? Keep a tally sheet at the desk and mark it before sending your customer off to hide their egg for the next person to find.

Video programs

If you have created a compilation of viral videos or other visual content, you can use that clicker to count every person in the room while the video is playing. Even casual viewers who tune in and out are benefiting in some way.

Craft tables and makerspaces

If your passive program is a "make it and take it" situation, ask staff to mark on a tally sheet whenever they observe customers using the resources.

You could also keep track of how many craft blanks get used. Put out the same amount each time so that you only need to tally the number of times you re-up the supplies.

Special spaces

If you implement one of the ideas you will find in our chapter on special spaces for passive programming, mark your tally sheet every time you see a customer interacting with your sensory station or taking advantage of your Chill Zone.

In a nutshell: strive to observe, count, and report every single interaction and engagement. If you're new to the passive programming game, it may take some time to develop this habit, but once you get the hang of it, it will become second nature, and the benefits to you and your library make it work the effort.

Sharing your successes

Do not be shy about self-promotion and branding. This is no time for modesty! Be proud of the creativity and energy you put into designing programs and the outcomes that result. Let your light shine, and increase public awareness of what you, your library, and libraries in general are all about.

Sure, social media can be toxic at times, but there's nothing like it for promoting, sharing, and stealing ideas. It lets you interact with librarians from around the world, inspire them with your projects, and be inspired by their projects. We've found that posts highlighting passive programs, especially, tend to generate lots of comments and "likes." It seems we are ALL looking for new and exciting low-key ways to engage our customers and broaden our reach. And sometimes you just want someone to commiserate with when a program fails to go as planned—librarians on social media are fantastic at offering support, suggestions, encouragement, and funny GIFs when you need them most.

You will find scores of library workers sharing their successes (and failures) on Twitter, Instagram, Pinterest, and Facebook groups such as Programming Librarian and Teen Services Underground.

Do not hesitate to share your successes in real life, too. When giving library tours to school groups, new employees, or visiting dignitaries, you want to point out your passive programming locations and explain exactly why you offer these kinds of activities and how they benefit your customers. During staff meetings and discussions with your supervisor, talk up your self-directed programs as much as your staff-led ones. Tell your coworkers from other departments about funny or endearing interactions you had as a result of these activities.

They may well follow your lead and start offering more passive programming, making your library into an engaging and interactive learning environment for all ages, and establishing you as an innovator and a leader.

Validate your passive programs with specific outcomes

Be aware of and able to articulate the specific skills and outcomes that result from various types of passive programs so you can justify offering them. It's not just a word search, it is a tool for building literacy, enhancing vocabulary, and teaching spelling! You are not rewarding young people for completing a maze, you are offering them incentives to develop problem-solving skills and sharpen executive function. You will find learning objectives for specific program ideas throughout this book.

Document, document, document

Document the results of all your passive programs. Stand on a chair and take a photo of the drawing table covered with doodles of sea creatures. Before you erase that chalkboard, take a picture of what your customers have contributed.

Any time you see a passive program outcome that makes you laugh or feel warm and fuzzy, photograph it for posterity. Flip through these pictures when you need inspiration for next month's plans, or when you're having a bad day and need a reminder of all the ways you have enriched your community. Images like these look great in a monthly report or on social media and provide visual evidence to support your statistics.

Take photos from several different angles, crop them, and adjust lighting if needed so your images are as clear, sharp, and impactful as possible. Your cell phone camera probably has the built-in capacity to do this, but there are plenty of photo editing apps that can really make your pictures pop. We like Snapseed for its ease of use and variety of editing options.

Media releases

Get permissions and media releases when you photograph customers, especially minors. Different systems manage media permissions in different ways. If yours requires signed paper forms, keep a batch ready at the desk for when you catch a customer interacting with your passive program in a particularly picturesque way.

One way to manage group events is to distribute release forms along with nametags as people walk in the door and then put a sticker on the nametag of any who don't want their picture shared. Later, when you're sorting through all the pictures of the event, only share the ones where you can see that everyone in them has a nametag without a sticker.

You can often get around the need for photo releases if you take photos that don't show the faces of minor children. With a bit of practice, you'll get the hang of composing interesting snapshots that feature only the back of a child's head and the project they are working on, or their little hand drawing on the chalkboard.

If you have a photo you just can't resist sharing, but no media release for the kid or kids in it, you might be able to post it anyway. If your photo editing skills are good enough, you can blur the faces or place an emoji sticker on top of their wee mug.

Lastly, whatever you do, don't post customers' names or any personal information on social media without their explicit permission—and even with permission, you should stay away from posting the names of minors.

Hashtag: #passiveprogramming

On social media, use a consistent hashtag for your programming posts, tag your system, and tag us! (We're @pwbalto and @airdna on Instagram; @pwbalto and @andriaamaral on Twitter.) We want to see what you've done! We probably want to steal it!

Consider creating a hashtag or separate account for your passive programming station. There are some mighty unlikely social media stars out there—who's to say your whiteboard can't be the next Instagram influencer?

It's not stealing if you give it away

Don't hoard your great ideas; share and make it easy for others to replicate them. Make PDFs of your craft instructions and other Word documents and convert them to JPG files for easier sharing on social media or Pinterest. Sharing ideas leads to collaboration, modification and enhanced programs. One of your followers may come up with a way to make your awesome concept even better, and your customers will reap the rewards when you offer the new and improved version.

INSTANT REPLAY:

"If you're too afraid to check your reflection in a mirror, start out by looking for your reflection in a book"

Response to writing prompt: what does the library mean to you?

Part II

Let the Games Begin: 101+ Passive Programming Ideas

Now that you know how to implement writing prompts, drawing prompts, polls, quizzes, and more using your bulletin board, whiteboard, table, Big Jar, or whatever resources you have; here are some specific ideas for you to adapt, ignore, or outright steal.

6

Game Plans: A Week of Wonder

Only the most ardent passive programmers will put out something new every day of the week, but it is a best practice to have at least one regular weekly passive program—and it is a great way to dip a toe into the practice. Frequent library visitors will begin to look for your Word of the Week writing prompt, or your Tuesday Zooday animal drawing challenge—whatever silly or serious passive program you decide to hang your hat on.

Doing this not only encourages engagement with the library, but it also invites customers to establish a library habit. It increases their comfort level and adds to their sense of ownership. When you see a kid come into your section and tell their friend, "It's Thursday! They always have a trivia quiz on Thursday!" it means you have given that child a little sense of mastery in your space, and put her in the position to teach another. And when a child thinks they are "good at" the library, that child can include the library in her list of assets, whether she needs help with homework, college or job applications, or leisure reading.

Take it up a level by offering easy and hard options—kids can master the easy version and then take a crack at the hard . . . and families can participate together, with the grownups working on the hard version while the children try the easy one. Leveled challenges are a familiar paradigm for anyone with experience playing video games, and they provide an intrinsic reward when the next level is conquered.

Whether you pick Tuesday Newsday or Trivia Thursday, here are some of our favorite alliterative and near-rhyming weekday events. Look in the Resources Appendix for some of our favorite print and online resources for these challenges.

Monday

Monday Fun Day

Mondays are hard for everyone, but some young people really struggle with sitting still all day after a weekend of freedom, and this can make them extra antsy. Start off the week with a physical challenge (or list six different challenges and provide a big die so they can roll to find out what to do), and set out books and videos about exercise and sports. Provide a timer for timed challenges. Start with these six ideas and look for more in our section on how to set up an Active Zone in our chapter on special spaces.

- Run in place for 30 seconds
- Do your favorite Fortnite dance
- Walk like a penguin to the wall and back
- S-T-R-E-T-C-H for 30 seconds
- Do as many pushups as you can
- Try a yoga pose

Media Monday

The weekly Best of the Web program at Andria's library is popular with teens but can be adapted for any age group. Put together a 15-minute YouTube playlist of entertaining and educational viral videos, connect a laptop to your monitor, set the playlist to repeat, and let it play for an hour.

Add an interactive element by setting up your whiteboard or putting out slips of paper for people to list their favorite viral videos or YouTubers. You can develop playlists around a theme or use the subject of an upcoming program for cross-promotion. Book trailers and previews of upcoming movies based on books are nice to include. Arguably the best part of Media Monday is that it lets staff ease into the work week with a good excuse for watching cat videos!

A-Maze-ing Monday (or Twisty Tuesday or Find Your Way Friday, or . . . you get the idea)

Photocopy easy (or challenging!) mazes from books by Roxie Munro or Sean Jackson (*From Here to There*), or find them online. Puzzlemaker.com is a good source.

Tuesday

Tuesday Newsday

Many news outlets create a weekly online multiple-choice current events quiz. The New York Times puts up a Weekly News Quiz for Students, but you can find lots of other options (see Appendix for resources).

Participants can work solo or in teams and consult Siri, Alexa, staff members, library materials, news sites, or other customers to find the answers.

There is no such thing as cheating when it comes to being well informed! We are right to teach young people to use all the resources at their disposal when seeking information. Along the way they will inevitably learn that some sources are more reliable than others. These quizzes create an opening for you to show them methods for evaluating sources and develop media literacy skills that are more essential now than ever.

You may be able to find an online quiz that suits your customers' age and ability perfectly, but chances are you'll want to copy, paste, and adapt some of the questions and answers. Your less news-savvy quiz takers will appreciate it if you create wrong answers that are silly and obvious. Your more internet-savvy quiz takers will not as readily find the online answer key if you change up the wording. Add pictures for extra appeal and to break up a wall of text.

Pick questions that appeal to local interests when possible and avoid ones that may trigger your customers. We don't use questions about school shootings or other events that include children in peril. Some weeks, this can be a bit of a challenge. If the news is full of atrocity and terror, look for anniversaries, sports, and culture questions.

Examples:

- What popular children's show is celebrating its 50th anniversary this week?
- What two teams are competing in the Super Bowl next week?
- Which of these foods is traditionally served on Chinese New Year?

Tuesday Zooday

Highlight a new animal once a week for your customers to try their hand at drawing. Make it a treasure hunt: offer rewards for facts, books, jokes, or YouTube videos about that animal, or hide pictures of the featured animal around the library. This is an easy one to support with materials from your collection. Animal books are one thing you can find in nearly every library!

Wednesday

Wacky Object Wednesday

Cindy Ritter at Greene County Library in Virginia puts one weird thing somewhere in the branch every Wednesday during summer reading. A sign at the reference desk challenges customers to find it. Glasses on the clock? Socks on the houseplant? A traffic cone just about anywhere in the library certainly qualifies as a wacky object. Kids who spot the out-of-context object get a little prize.

What will you hide in your library? A blender in the fiction section? A rubber chicken? This is a great way to draw people into areas they might not usually explore, where they may discover materials they didn't even know they needed.

Where in the world? Wednesday

There's a town in Texas named Oatmeal—but a lot of people probably don't know that. Post the name of an obscure town or remote geographic feature and reward the folks who can locate it. This activity offers great practice at using an atlas (put some out on display!) or Google Maps and gives you the opportunity to demonstrate how to use those resources.

Word Search Wednesday

There are lots of websites that will generate a custom word search based on a word list and grid size that you supply. Our favorite as of this writing is puzzlemaker.com—it produces word searches in a font that is easy to process visually and can be simply pasted into Word documents, and it automatically prevents inappropriate words from being formed by accident. Nothing causes a ruckus quite like a stray cussword embedded in an otherwise innocent word puzzle.

Whatever site you use, here are some fun ideas for word search themes that go beyond the usual seasonal options:

- Use words that tie into the theme of other library programs for a quick shot of cross-promotion.
- Make a list that celebrates the arrival of the newest entry in a hot book series—the dragons of *Wings of Fire*, for example.
- Enhance users' vocabulary by creating a word search where all the words are synonymous.
- Shock your kid and teen customers with the depth of your gamer knowledge by making word searches full of jargon from Minecraft, Roblox, Fortnight, Overwatch, or whatever game is currently causing mass hysteria at your computers.
- For bonus points, make a puzzle where the letters that are left over after finding all the words spell out a secret message (Puzzlemaker.com offers this option).

Thursday

Trivia Thursday

Google can help you find a list of trivia questions and answers on nearly any topic you can imagine, and there are many ways to implement a trivia contest using whatever space you have.

Display books of general knowledge, almanacs, and *Ripley's Believe It or Not*, or just add the call number for this section to your answer sheets. If your trivia questions are all based on a theme like Women's History Month, display reference and nonfiction books relating to that subject.

Tips:

- Be sure the questions match the age and sophistication level of your customers—for example, don't put a question about Zsa Zsa Gabor on any quiz directed at people under 60 years old.
- Have a nonlibrarian friend or teen test drive any trivia quiz to quickly identify any extra-difficult questions or, perhaps more importantly, any questions that will lead to terrible internet pitfalls.
- If a participant finds an answer that differs from the one on your answer key, have them show you how and where they found the information. Sometimes there are conflicting facts out there. Sometimes they searched correctly but interpreted the information wrong. In either of these cases, give them their prize anyway, and take advantage of the opportunity to lay down some information literacy.
- Rewording the questions even slightly from how they appear online will reduce the chances of your searchers' Google results leading them directly to the site from which you took your trivia questions.

Thursday = Thor's Day

Post a word or phrase with its translation into other languages (don't forget American Sign Language!) and pronunciation. Customers who try out their new word or phrase on a staff member get a sticker or other tiny prize.

Friday

Freaky Fact Friday

Bizarre facts and weird news stories are endlessly amusing, appeal to all ages, and can be used for passive programs in a variety of ways. Hide eggs filled with freaky facts around your library for customers to find and share with staff. Or set it up "two truths and a lie" style: grab a couple of unlikely headlines and display them along with something from satirical news site *The Onion*—or just make something up yourself. Participants have to guess which one is false.

Make up an activity sheet for this one, or turn it into a poll for your bulletin board, chalkboard, or voting method of choice. Display books and other resources about media literacy, fake news, and hoaxes.

At Andria's library, News of the Weird is a popular diversion. Six different unusual headlines are posted on a board, along with QR codes leading to the actual news story online. Teens use sticker dots to vote for their favorite of the posted news items, and they get a small prize for finding another weird news story online (from a credible source only) and turning it in to library staff. It's led to many delightful conversations about unexpected topics and is a sneaky way to develop young people's information literacy.

Friday favorites

Even the most energetic of us can find ourselves exhausted by the end of the week, and there's no shame in admitting you need something you can put together with a minimum of effort. Many libraries are also short-staffed on Fridays, so an activity that requires staff to check worksheets or give out prizes simply may not be practical. Also, your customers may not be up for deep thinking or complex games by the time Friday rolls around.

This makes Friday a great time to put out a poll. Use your vertical space or Big Jar to ask customers the big questions: "What's the best kind of cheese?" "Cat or dog?" "Pineapple on pizza, yes or no?"

Saturday

Shopping Saturday

Does your library pull the advertising circulars out of its newspapers? Save them up and put them out once a week along with a shopping list worksheet: "You've got $50 to spend at the store. What do you buy? How much change will you have?" Leave this open, or specify a purpose: you're buying supplies for a picnic, a party, a trip to outer space—or to build a robot.

It can be a lot of fun to see what people buy with their pretend money. "Fifty bucks worth of shaving cream and a box of trash bags? Just what exactly are you planning?!" There's nothing more delightful than an eight-year-old laughing maniacally.

Librarians put a lot of energy into literacy, but numeracy can be learned at the library, too.

Sounds Good Saturday

Here's a great prompt that captures even the quick-stop user who's just running in to pick up their holds on Saturday. Park an easel with a whiteboard by the checkout that asks: What are you listening to?

More ideas to adapt to your schedule

Word of the week

Post your chosen word and its definition, and challenge customers to write a sentence that includes it. Or post an unusual word and invite speculation on what it could mean. "Antediluvian" is, like, a class of turtles, right?

What's in the jar?

Put a withdrawn book or scrap paper through the paper shredder and stuff the shreds in a Big Jar. Then, once a week, nestle a small object in the middle of the jar so that it can't be seen from outside. Provide slips for customers to guess the object in the jar, or let them write their answers on your whiteboard/chalkboard.

This seemingly impossible challenge can be cracked a number of ways. Post a new hint every day. Or offer your guessers opportunities to "earn" extra hints or the chance to ask yes or no questions: double your stats by having them complete another passive program challenge to earn their hints or questions. Alternatively, use an egg timer and let guessers write down as many objects as they can think of until the time runs out. Next week, display the hidden object alongside a brand-new challenge.

Have fun with this: pick an object with local or current events relevance, or pick a small object that is usually in plain sight. "What's missing from the reference desk?"

Take your best guess

Fill your big jar with candies, LEGO, marbles, or any other small objects. Participants try to guess the number of items. Combining objects of various sizes in one jar ups the challenge. If the winner is going to get all the candy in the jar, use individually wrapped sweets. You don't want to give away a bag of jelly beans after you've touched each one to count it!

INSTANT REPLAY:

A 7th grade boy gives an incorrect answer to his Women's History Month trivia question.

Me: "Sorry, the answer is Phillis Wheatley."

Him: "oh, man, that's what Kayla told me to say. I should have listened to her."

Me: "So, what did we learn here today?"

Him: "That women are always right."

Me: "I will accept that answer. You can have a piece of candy."

7

You Make the Call: Themes and Ideas to Try Any Time of Year

Whatever you're in the mood for, there's a passive program to match. Pick at random from this section, tweak it to fit your needs, or select a theme and make it Whatever Month at your library. Don't forget, though: if something's not working, switch it up. That's the beauty of passive programming. You can always adapt the elements, try it again at another time, or discard it entirely, never to be spoken of again.

We're going to start with ideas based on libraries and books and end with pop culture and assorted silliness.

Learn your library—love your library

Start with what you know: your library. Scavenger hunts, bingo cards, and other library-centric activities increase customers' familiarity with your materials, services, and staff while also sharpening their observation skills and building vocabulary. They're an easy way to draw attention to new or little-used features of your library, AND if one of the activities on the list requires participants to interact with another of your passive programs, you just doubled your stats. Good job! Once you've developed something that works well in your environment, you will want to have a stash of instructions already printed and ready to go. They will come in handy when a school group shows up unannounced.

Library scavenger hunts

Scavenger hunts work even when you have no space at all for passive programming. You'll find scavenger hunts themed to various heritage months and holidays throughout our chapter on a year of passive programming. Here are a few that are library specific and can be implemented any time of year.

Shopping list

Post a sign or print scavenger hunt sheets asking participants to find examples of items in specific categories: a newspaper from another state, a nonfiction book about art, a DVD about sports, a children's book written in another language, a novel by Stephen King, a New Book with a blue cover, and so on. Participants will collect these items and return them with their scavenger hunt lists.

Where is it?

Take pictures of library fixtures for customers to find. The storytime rug, the listening station, the self-checkout, computer sign-up station, the biography section, and any permanent art installations are all good options. Print these pictures on a scavenger hunt sheet alongside a checkbox. This is a great option for pre-readers to do with their families and perfect for field trip visits. Older children and teens could be asked to write the location where they found the item, for extra literacy skill building.

A fun variation on this is to include a library staff member in each picture. Tyaisha Boyd at Enoch Pratt Free Library took pictures of her branch's beloved security guard, Officer Jones, posing in front of various shelves in the library.

Challenge library users to label each picture with the section of the library it depicts or make a match game by listing the shelving locations pictured. Players will have to scrutinize the materials in the background of each photo carefully in order to figure out if the staff member is hanging out in the craft section, among the mysteries, or with the graphic novels.

You might try this with action shots—"catch" a library staff member browsing the newspaper collection, relaxing in a comfy chair, checking out her books, and so on. Or try it with a stuffed toy or the library mascot instead.

One of These Things Is Not Like the Others

This single-item scavenger hunt challenges visitors to scour the library looking for an object that has no business being there. Stash a blender at the end of a fiction shelf or a fancy high-heeled shoe in with the cookbooks. Why is there a bowling trophy on top of the print station? Participants will leave the item where it is and just tell a staff member where they found it.

Pick an object big enough to stand out and unusual enough that there's no conceivable reason for it to be in the library. You'll also find this idea in our chapter on a week of passive programming, inspired by Wacky Object Wednesday at Greene County Library in Virginia.

Library bingo

Ask participants to complete small tasks in various library departments to get a stamp for their bingo card. Tasks can be as simple as "introduce yourself to the Reference Librarian" and "visit the Local History room," or more skill based, like "locate the call number for books about astronomy." Create two levels of bingo cards (beginner and expert) for a program that engages customers of all ages, and don't forget to include squares on the bingo card that direct customers to engage with other passive programs in the building!

Fact-finding missions

This differs from a scavenger hunt in that participants answer questions about the library instead of collecting or locating items. Create a quick quiz that requires customers to walk around the library, noticing things they may have missed. For instance: who painted the landscape hanging in the lobby? What movie is being shown on the 23rd of this month? What's the subject of the display in the teen area? What is the library book club reading next?

Match the selfie to the shelfie

There are a LOT of different interpretations of this game. All encourage library users to match photos of people with pictures that illustrate their reading preferences. Provide an entry form for customers to fill out and drop in a contest box for a drawing or provide instant gratification by posting a lift-the-flap hidden answer key.

Staff favorites

The simplest (but possibly most challenging) version of this program asks library customers to match photos of library staff with the cover of their favorite book, or the book they're currently reading. Alternatively, ask staff to take and share a picture of their home bookshelf—or their favorite section of the library—along with a selfie. Post the numbered pictures and make an entry form or answer key.

Either way, this concept is great for bulletin boards in small or school libraries with lots of repeat customers and can help users to learn staffers' names and recognize those who share their reading preferences, so they know who to approach when they want a recommendation.

Pop culture shelfies

Search the web for photos of the home libraries of famous people. Then set up a match game between celebrity headshots and their bookshelves.

You can even do this with fictional characters. Here are some movie libraries and the characters who use them that make for an easy match game:

TABLE 7.1

Character	Library
1. Hermione Granger	A. The Hogwarts Library
2. Tom Hanks in *The Da Vinci Code*	B. Vatican Library
3. Sherlock Holmes	C. Bookshelf at Baker Street
4. Lincoln Rhymes	D. Home Library from *The Bone Collector*
5. Belle	E. The Beast's Library

Library clue

This is time consuming to set up but worth it if your customers buy in, as it incorporates recursive elements, requires multiple return visits, and develops critical thinking skills. It's ideal for school and academic libraries with established customers who are frequent visitors, and it has wide appeal. Who doesn't want to solve a mystery?

Invent a murder that took place at the library and identify members of your staff as potential culprits. We think it is a bit grim and unsettling to designate a real live person as a murder victim, so we suggest you invent a character for that role.

Your bulletin board makes a good home base for this program. Post photos of the suspects along with made-up names. Follow the Clue naming tradition by calling them "Librarian Lemon," "Professor Green," "Madame Magenta," and so on, and frame the photos with the corresponding color. Display a map of the library and the fictional scenario along with the photos. Provide sheets listing the rooms, weapons, and suspects. Use the board game as a template and inspiration but customize it to your setting.

Once a week, release new information that eliminates some choices. Continue releasing info until the last week, when the entire scenario is revealed. As soon as participants think they know the solution, they can write it up and turn it in. Everyone who submits a solution before the answer is revealed will be entered in a drawing for prizes, or you can select a winner at random from among those who correctly solved the mystery.

Supplement this with a display of murder mysteries, especially *In the Hall with the Knife* by Diana Peterfreund.

Customer feedback

Passive programs can give your customers a space to express their opinions about the library and shows that you welcome the feedback and value their input. In the process you gain critical information you can use to develop and fine-tune the services you offer your community. You can set up a good old-fashioned suggestion box, create surveys that target specific user groups and service areas, or put writing prompts in a public space like a whiteboard. This is an excellent strategy for any outreach events as it will provide insight into the thoughts and feelings of any in attendance who may not yet be regular library users.

Some sample questions include:

- Why do you love your library?
- What is your favorite part of the library?
- What do you wish the library had?
- What prevents you from using the library more often?
- Vote: What's your favorite thing about the library: fun activities/great books/ friendly people/access to technology, and so on?

If you're struggling to plan events that teens in your community will attend, use your whiteboard to ask "what special program should we do next?" Give a few examples they can vote for and leave plenty of space for them to add their own. This will generate ideas that may never have occurred to you and allows teens to indicate enthusiasm for others' suggestions by underlining, circling or writing "YASSSSSSS" next to their favorites.

At the Booth and Dimock Memorial Library in Coventry, Connecticut, members of the Tween Advisory Board surprised staffers Meg Cavicchi and Kayla Fontaine by answering this question with the enigmatic "toast party." They later clarified this meant eating toast "with all sorts of toppings." Meg and Kayla shrugged and brought in toasters, bread, a variety of spreads, and the toast party ended up being one of their most popular tween programs. Who'd have thought?

"I love my library because" is a great writing prompt for any time.

All about the books

Passport programs

Everyone knows about Summer Reading, but Passport programs can be adapted and implemented on a smaller scale any time of the year. They keep those pages turning and help broaden reading tastes while allowing plenty of freedom to choose.

Whether you provide a list of suggested titles or not (and lists can be very helpful, especially for programs aimed at kids), don't be too picky about the books readers choose. Do all the books that they read for the program strictly adhere to the guidelines? Who cares! They went through the process of selection, evaluation, and reading—this is a win.

Passport programs, by the way, are ideal partnership opportunities. They fit what people expect from a library, and it's not hard to get sponsors to buy into the goal of encouraging lifelong literacy. The printed material allows for the placement of branding and logos without looking too "advertise-y," and the prizes can be provided by the partner, easing the burden on your budget.

Baltimore City's library system partners with the National Aquarium on a passport program called Read to Reef. Children get a special bookmark on which they record aquatic-themed books they've read. When they have finished five titles, they can take the bookmark directly to the Aquarium for four free tickets.

Sports teams, museums, county park systems, zoos, and other local attractions are great candidates for partner programs like this.

But even without a partner, passport programs are fun self-paced challenges. Here are just a few ideas.

Jack of all genres

Challenge customers to read a mystery, a thriller, a sci-fi novel, a fantasy, a romance, a Western, and so on. You might just find a new favorite!

Book bingo

Create a bingo card with different genres, formats, and authors. You can offer two levels of prizes, one for getting "bingo" and another for completing the entire card.

Year-round reading

Lots of passport and other library offerings are intended to draw in new users or encourage nonreaders, but a year-round reading program plays to our base. This one is for the capital-R Readers in your community.

Roll it out in January and promote it all year. Challenge readers to explore different subjects and formats. You can make a checklist that people have to complete by the end of the year, or you can designate specific themes for each month. Tie it in with your existing monthly themes. If you always do a Jewish American Heritage Month display, make "read a book relevant to the Jewish experience" a May challenge.

Sites like Book Riot and Popsugar post an annual reading challenge. Mine these and other challenges for inspiration (we love the Rory Gilmore Reading Challenge—did you know that Rory was seen reading 339 books on screen?). Just be sure to credit them and include their logo and URL on your materials. We've listed a few options in the Appendix.

Themed reading

Supplement your monthly themes and get those books moving off your displays with a monthlong reading challenge like "how many poems can you read this April?" or "read 3 books by African-American authors this February."

CLEVER KIDS AROUND the WORLD

Folktales featuring young people outwitting giants, ogres, witches, and the like are found in nearly every culture on earth and empower children to face their fears.

Fearsome Giant, Fearless Child by Paul Fleischman
Clever Beatrice by Margaret Willey
Thumbelina by Jerry Pinkney
Odd and the Frost Giants by Neil Gaiman
Mighty Jack by Ben Hatke
Baba Yaga's Assistant by Marika McCoola
The Talking Eggs by Robert D. San Souci
Sam and the Tigers: A Retelling of Little Black Sambo by Julius Lester and Jerry Pinkney

FAIRY TALES RETOLD

There is no shortage of retellings of the most common fairy tales, and many have cultural variants. Young children delight in hearing or reading a familiar story with an unexpected twist. Recognizing the story boosts their confidence as readers, the new elements spark their creativity. Challenge young readers to explore different versions of well-known tales. Include graphic novel versions to expose them to different formats.

Goldilocks

Goldilocks and the Three Dinosaurs by Mo Willems

The Ghanaian Goldilocks by Tamara Pizzoli

Goldilocks and Just One Bear by Leigh Hodgkinson

The Goldilocks Variations by Allan Ahlberg

Yours Truly, Goldilocks by Alma Flor Ada

And classic tellings of Goldilocks by, Lauren Child, Margaret Willey, James Marshall

Red Riding Hood

Ninja Red Riding Hood by Corey Rosen Schwartz

Pretty Salma by Niki Daly

Little Red and the Very Hungry Lion by Alex T. Smith

Petite Rouge by Mike Artell

Little Roja Riding Hood by Susan Middleton Elya

Wolf in the Snow by Matthew Cordell

Lon Po Po by Ed Young

And classic versions by Jerry Pinkney, Trina Schart Hyman, and others

Cinderella

Glass Slipper, Gold Sandal by Paul Fleischman

Yeh-Shen by Ai-Ling Louie

Adelita by Tomie DePaola

Mufaro's Beautiful Daughters by John Steptoe

The Golden Sandal by Rebecca Hickox

Jouanah: A Hmong Cinderella by Jewell Reinhart Coburn

Abadeha: The Philippine Cinderella by Myrna J. de la Paz

Anklet for a Princess: A Cinderella Story from India by Lila Mehta

The Gift of the Crocodile by Judy Sierra

The Way Meat Loves Salt by Nina Jaffe

Little Gold Star: A Spanish American Cinderella Tale by Robert D. San Souci

The Irish Cinderlad by Shirley Climo

Cendrillon by Robert D. San Souci

The Rough-Face Girl by Rafe Martin

Interstellar Cinderella by Deborah Underwood

TALL TALES

Look for stories about Paul Bunyan, Pecos Bill, Bigfoot Wallace, Finn McCool, Old Stormalong, Mike Fink, Thunder Rose, and the classic tall tale and story starter *I Was Born about 10,000 Years Ago* by Steven Kellogg.

Baby

1,000 Books before kindergarten

Many library systems implement this passport program. It's a great way to establish the reading habit with new parents, and it keeps them coming back to the library. Take advantage of those visits by promoting adult programs and services as well as storytimes and other children's programming.

Be sure you support your library's 1,000 Books program with passive programming that rewards parents and kids.

Make a mobile or garland for peer recommendations: "Lucas and I loved *Chugga Chugga Choo Choo!*" Throw up periodic polls on your whiteboard or chalkboard so that caregivers can express their preference for Ezra Jack Keats or Vera Williams.

Post progress sheets and update them with stickers at each milestone. Families that complete the program should have the opportunity for visual recognition. If they agree to it, take a cell phone photo, print it out, and display it in a construction paper frame.

Book to art

Give your craft table or art cart some literary inspiration. Look for picture books and graphic novels created with easily reproducible art techniques or ideas that extend into the real world and use them as a starting point. Lois Ehlert's Leaf Man is a classic example, and we'll showcase this celebration of autumn color in our Year of Passive Programs chapter. Here are some other ideas, inspired by Maryland librarian Kelsey Harper.

Note: You'll want to have the book on hand in order to provide visual reference—we suggest making color copies of relevant pages so that the book itself doesn't end up getting drawn on by little hands. Laminate those copies or put them in sign holders so they don't get lost, torn, or grubby. And of course you'll have copies of the book available for checkout, right?

It looked like spilled milk

Clouds can take on any shape—we've used this book to inspire a whiteboard prompt ("I once saw a cloud that looked like . . .") and as a very messy librarian-led program involving paint and string. For your craft table, print out a variety of cloud pictures in black and white, or sketch cloud shapes on your drawing table, and provide markers for embellishment. "What does this cloud look like to you? Draw in details to make it unmistakable!"

Ekua Holmes/Brian Collier collage

Collage art can feel less intimidating to some people because there's little to no drawing involved. Pull out a bin of photo-heavy magazines (finally something to do with those *National Geographics* that everyone insists on donating!), provide scissors and glue sticks, and see what comes forth.

Ed Emberley's thumbprints

Stamp pads are found in every library, so this one is easy-peasy. Set some out on your craft table with examples from Emberley's books and markers for adding details. Don't forget to set out baby wipes for cleanup, so you don't find smudgy, inky fingerprints all over the library!

Joyce Hesselberth's shapes

A triangle for a face, a circle for the body, and skinny rectangles for limbs—can you make characters using just geometric shapes? Cut out shapes in lots of different sizes and colors, set out glue sticks and blank paper, and let customers try their hand at creating characters and scenes. Use a paper cutter and circular punches if you have them to make setup for this craft table activity easier.

This also works on a magnetic whiteboard—this method is considerably easier to keep supplied . You only have to cut one set of shapes, laminate them, and stick a magnet on the back of each. They can be rearranged endlessly.

Not a Box by Antoinette Portis

Anyone can draw a box, right? And everyone knows that a box can also be a spaceship, a race car, or a burning building. What else can you draw, starting with a picture of a box? This is a fine craft table activity that works on a whiteboard as well. Use permanent markers to draw a variety of boxes. Customers can add the details in erasable marker.

Note: Don't worry, permanent marker on whiteboard isn't the end of the world. Hand sanitizer will take it right off.

E! Emergency! by Tom Lichtenheld

Letters have personalities, as we all know. Get practice learning to draw them, and give them faces, clothes, expressions, and stories. Try using large letter stencils on the craft table or board for children and provide examples of chunky lettering for teens and adults.

Activity sheets

Book to character match game

For younger children, use illustrations of characters from picture books. Pick Olivia, Peppa Pig, and Mercy Watson for a pig-themed match game, or pick books in which the illustration style is distinctive and the match between cover and character will be fairly obvious—remember, not all families will be familiar with the Western picture book canon. This activity is a great visual literacy exercise.

Here are some illustrators with strongly distinctive styles:

Sophie Blackall
Eric Carle
Ekua Holmes
Molly Idle
Yuyi Morales
LeUyen Pham
Sean Qualls
Suzy Lee
Raul the Third
Erin Stead

Older children and teens can be challenged with graphic novel and series fiction characters. Make this program extra hard for adults by using characters from classic and popular fiction.

Books in disguise

Can you identify a book from only the cover? Download the cover art of popular titles and paste them into Publisher or your preferred image creating software. Draw black boxes over the title and author or use image editing software to blur out identifying text.

Print and post these images as an activity sheet (although this also works on a whiteboard or bulletin board). Challenge participants to give the title or author of each.

A slightly insane variation on this takes advantage of your library's stash of LEGOs. Use a website such as Bricapic or Legoizer to convert a book cover image to a schematic for composing the cover image—IN LEGO. Set a couple of these up as LEGO challenges for your best builders; then display the resulting work prominently and invite guesses as to what book it represents.

Word searches

Make a puzzle using names of characters and places in a well-known book or series. Or try this with author names, one-word titles, or book terms (spine, page, endpaper, etc.).

Reading reaction!

Here's a great version of Match the Selfie to the Shelfie that can be adapted for all ages and collections. Take pictures of one staff member miming a variety of exaggerated reactions—surprised, terrified, laughing, sneaky, thinking—while reading a book. Make sure the book covers don't show in the photos.

Print the pictures alongside the covers of books that correspond to the expressions. Or set up this match game on a bulletin board, wall, or whiteboard. Players have to match the look on the librarian's face with the book they might be reading. Note: there are no wrong answers.

Some books that match reactions for kids:

Surprise—*Ripley's Believe it or Not*
Fear—*Goosebumps* by R.L. Stine
Laughing—*Dog Man* by Dav Pilkey
Sneaky—*Spy School* by Stuart Gibbs
Thinking—any DK Eyewitness book

For adults, you can add a few additional reactions:

Surprise—*Guinness Book of World Records*
Fear—a book by Paul Tremblay, Nick Cutter or Stephen King
Laughing—a book by a comedian like Ali Wong or Phoebe Robinson
Sneaky—a heist novel by Donald E. Westlake
Thinking—*A Brief History of the Universe* by Stephen Hawking
Sad—*Beloved* by Toni Morrison
Serene—a book on meditation
Sexy—anything by Christina Lauren or Nikki Turner

Writing/drawing prompts

Book-related prompts like these tend to be added to little by little, until your board is a beautiful mess of writing. For that reason, it's worth keeping them up a long time. If you have a window or a glass partition wall, think about making it a recommendation prompt or a wonderful words window for as long as a month or two. Someone will invariably contribute a swear word or a drawing of a penis during that time—see if you can wipe those out without disturbing the entire installation.

- Share a line from a book that struck you as memorable in some way.
- What book (or video game) would you like to see made into a movie? (And who do you want to see cast in it?)
- What book (or movie) would you like to live in?
- What fictional character would you want to date/be friends with?

- My favorite literary character is. . . .
- What Olympic sport would your favorite character medal in?
- What should I read next?

Genre Jar

A repository for staff recommendations and peer recommendations alike, the Genre Jar (or Barrel of Books, Box of Best Books) contains book titles printed on slips of colored paper—purple for mystery, pink for romance, green for sci-fi, and so on. This is great for people who are looking for book suggestions but are shy about asking library staff.

Leave blank slips by the jar so that readers can make their own contributions.

Book suggestions are color coded according to genre in the teen department at Baltimore's Southeast Anchor Library.

Your Genre Jar might be a bulletin board or a shelf—whatever works for your space.

Gabbi Pace, a library worker in Charleston, South Carolina, used this method to create an interactive display titled "branch out into a new genre." A fishbowl contained construction paper leaf shapes on which different genres were written. The book display was divided by genres. Readers selected a leaf at random and then browsed the corresponding section of the display to find a title from that genre that appealed to them.

Find a book infographic

Use flowchart software or a graphics program like Microsoft Publisher to create an infographic that asks readers to make choices that will lead them to their perfect book. We've seen these for supernatural YA, graphic novels, and diverse books. This can be time consuming but fun to devise, and it makes a great handout at school visits and outreach events.

Recommendation prompts

Reader-contributed recommendations are solid gold. Make extra sure you document the results of recommendation prompts, so that you can create booklists or displays. And don't be shy about announcing that your new booklist or display is entirely made up of books recommended by users of *this* library.

I can't wait for the next . . .

What has George R. R. Martin been doooooing all this time?? Share your love for your favorite book series.

I did *not* see that coming!

The poison was in the glass (*Justified*)! They're doing brain transplants (*Get Out*)! She had an identical twin (*A Simple Favor*)! He was dead all along (*The Sixth Sense*)! What book or movie had the twistiest plot twist you've ever come across?

Here are some other ideas to get the ball rolling:

- Tell us the scariest book you've ever read!
- What's the last book you read that made you:
  - . . . laugh out loud?
  - . . . fall in love?
  - . . . stay up way too late?
  - . . . reach for the tissues?

Poll/voting

Date/Marry/Kill

Pick three well-known literary characters and see what your library folks think of them. If we had to pick from Khal Drogo, Sherlock Holmes, or Easy Rawlins . . . well, actually we wouldn't marry any of those guys.

Shredded books

Here are some great ways to squeeze a little additional life out of those loved-to-pieces titles you hate to discard.

Book in a Jar

When a popular title is weeded for condition, cut its pages into horizontal strips ½–1" wide (use a paper cutter, for pity's sake—don't ruin the "good" scissors!), and put them in a jar. Customers try to guess the title of the book from the words they can read on the strips. Guesses go in an Enter to Win jar.

Depending on the book you choose and how you pack the jar, this can be a very difficult contest. Try to find books with characters whose names are unusual and well known (*The Hobbit*, Harry Potter, or *The Hunger Games* are good choices), or that have distinctive illustrations. Make sure there are some strips visible that give solid clues.

Including the sliced-up cover of a paperback or the dust jacket of a hard-cover can also decrease the degree of difficulty.

Books in Bits match game

This variation of Book in a Jar is a bit less challenging. Accumulate a few popular titles that have been weeded from your collection. Cut the pages into strips and put the shreds of each book in a separate zip-top bag. Provide the titles and challenge your customers to match each bag of book shreds to its title. In the children's department, choose graphic novels and well-known picture books. For teens and adults, pick books with recognizable proper names.

Inclusivity

Passive programming is a great way to reach out and embrace library visitors that regular active programs fail to entice. We try to make all our programs welcoming to everyone, but we seldom have the resources to present them in every customer's native language, or with modifications that make them accessible to the full range of neurological or physical ability.

Here's your chance to make everyone feel seen. If you have a significant—or even not so significant—population of speakers of another language in your community, make sure your passive programming is available in that language as well as English. You may have someone on staff who can help translate, or use Google Translate or a translation app such as Say Hi as a last resort.

Investigate cultural observances—if you know there are a lot of Korean Americans who visit your library, devise passive programs for Chu Suk and National Foundation Day, and show those customers that you see and welcome them.

You might even want to dedicate a board or table to activities only in Spanish, *por ejemplo*. Your Spanish-speaking customers will be delighted to find something just for them when they come to the library.

Writing and recommendation prompts

I learned about _____ people when I read (or watched) _____

TABLE 7.2

Identity	Example title
Chilean	*I Lived on Butterfly Hill* by Marjorie Agosin
Cherokee	*We Are Grateful: Otsaliheliga* by Traci Sorell
Sudanese	*The Red Pencil* by Andrea Pinkney
Nonbinary	*I Wish You All the Best* by Mason Deaver
Somali refugees	*When Stars Are Scattered* by Victoria Jamieson and Omar Mohamed
Kids with really long names	*Alma and How She Got Her Name* by Juana Martinez-Neal
People who have panic attacks	*Anger Is a Gift* by Mark Oshiro
Trans girls	*George* by Alex Gino
People with physical disability	*Not So Different: What You Really Want to Ask about Having a Disability* by Shane Burcaw

Here's a beautiful way for customers to share books about people from cultures different from their own or people with physical or neurological challenges. Draw a grid (use skinny washi tape to make straight lines!) and fill in the first couple rows yourself. We've provided a few examples in Table 7.2.

Supplement this prompt with a display of new and classic books that serve as windows to the diversity of human experience. There are simply too many to list here, but the books recognized by the Schneider Family Book Award and www.weneeddiversebooks.com are great places to start.

What's a question you wish people would ask you?

Post this writing prompt one week, and follow it up the next week with, "What's a question you wish people would STOP asking you?"

What wrong assumption do people make about you?

Confront prejudice head on with this hard-hitting question and be prepared for insightful and possibly heart-rending replies.

Translate your name

We love this as an easy-to-implement visceral experience of trying on how other people communicate. In our chapter: A Year of Passive Programming, we pair it with holidays and heritage months from around the world.

Your name in ASL

Post the American Sign Language alphabet on your board, display sign language books, or post links to YouTube sign language dictionary channels. Challenge customers to learn how to sign their name and introduce themselves to a staff member in sign language. Encourage staff to learn to respond, "Hi, ____! My name is Andria! I'm happy to see you!"

If you've got a monitor, you can play videos of picture books with simultaneous ASL translation. Try YouTube channels ASLIzed and ERCODvideos or use the Sign Language Storytelling Series from Weston Woods.

Find your Ghanaian name

Names in some parts of the world are based on birthdate. Provide a perpetual calendar and a chart so that customers can discover their Ashanti Twi day name. You'll find a link in the Appendix.

Write your name in another alphabet

Provide samples of Hebrew, Cyrillic, and Greek alphabets and challenge people to translate their first names. Not all scripts lend themselves to direct transliteration—challenge yourself to make this work with Hindi, Tagalog, or Cherokee. See the Resources Appendix for online resources.

Current events

Passive programs can educate customers about the world around them, encourage civic participation, and promote media literacy and pop culture awareness.

Writing prompts

- What current event worries you the most?
- What current event gives you the most hope for the future?
- How will you change the world?

Pair this with a display of books about young people taking action. Some titles to feature:

10 Things I Can Do to Help My World by Melanie Walsh

Through My Eyes by Ruby Bridges

Follow the Moon Home: A Tale of One Idea, Twenty Kids, and a Hundred Sea Turtles by Philippe Cousteau

The Boys Who Challenged Hitler: Knud Pedersen and the Churchill Club by Phillip Hoose

The Boy Who Harnessed the Wind by William Kamkwamba

Turning 15 on the Road to Freedom: My Story of the Selma Voting Rights March by Lynda Blackmon Lowery

Kid Activists: True Tales of Childhood from Champions of Change by Robin Stevenson

No One Is Too Small to Make a Difference by Greta Thunberg

Separate is Never Equal: Sylvia Mendez and Her Family's Fight for Desegregation by Duncan Tonatiuh

One Peace: True Stories of Young Activists by Janet Wilson

Malala's Magic Pencil by Malala Yousafzai

Vote

Issues poll

The Newseum in Washington, DC, always has a poll posted at the entrance. Museum visitors vote using sticker dots on questions like, "Do you think immigration restrictions keep us safe?" or "Have the presidential debates changed your mind on how you will vote?"

News of the weird

Post a number of weird but true news stories. Vote for your favorite! Extra credit for customers who find their own weird stories from reputable news sources. You'll find online sources for kooky news stories in the Appendix— lots of people collect and aggregate Man Bites Dog stories.

Mock election

Take the pulse of your community by posting your own poll querying customers on local or national candidates and issues.

Activity sheets

Current events make for great regularly scheduled passive programs. You'll find Tuesday Newsday and Freaky Fact Friday in our chapter on A Week of Passive Programming.

Fake or fact

Media literacy is a crucial skill and becoming more important all the time. Unfortunately, study after study (as well as our own experience administering current events quizzes) shows that many people are very bad at distinguishing substantiated news from made-up reporting. Give 'em some practice with a low stakes, fun quiz.

Copy headlines from a number of news stories from a variety of sources. Include legitimate news outlets, but also copy headlines from news satire sites like the *Onion* and *Weekly World News* and satire columns like "The Borowitz Report" in *New York Magazine*. This works best when all the stories revolve around the same topic—global warming, a sports cheating scandal, or technology news work well in this context. Set this up as a true/false or multiple-choice quiz. Which stories are legit and which don't pass the sniff test?

Best of the web

If you have access to a big screen in the library, keep it lively with a YouTube playlist of relevant, interesting, and amusing viral videos. Provide a whiteboard, a suggestion box, or other means for library users to submit their favorite videos for future compilations.

Cards and letters

Grassroots community activism programs often use letter writing campaigns to increase awareness and lobby for action. Is a group in your area agitating for a new park? Are after-school programs in danger of losing funding? Keep your ear to the ground for opportunities to participate in community discourse and promote civic engagement.

Or make your letter writing table a place for people to write encouraging cards and letters to military service members (Support Our Troops or Operation Gratitude), refugees (CARE Letters of Hope, Letters of Love Foundation), children living in poverty (Save the Children), or others. Web addresses for these campaigns are in the Appendix.

Supplies such as pens, pencils, and stationery are helpful, as well as templates for letter writing. Templates and other supporting materials may be available online. Use a box or basket to collect the completed cards and letters.

Adults as well as kids will gain practice using persuasive or expressive language, along with proper correspondence formats.

Self-expression

Passive programs can give your customers a chance to explore, express, and celebrate what makes them unique. This provides teens, especially, the opportunity to do the identity work that is so crucial to their stage of development—but all ages benefit from exercises in self-definition.

Writing/art prompts

Writing and drawing prompts have the added benefit of being exceptionally quick to put up. Keep a large selection of these self-expression questions in your back pocket. They're great ways to use your chalkboard or whiteboard between scheduled programs—and to keep traffic flowing to that spot.

Use a whiteboard on an easel to add a self-expression question to any event that draws a crowd. It's a great conversation starter and gives you a chance to make visitors feel valued and cared for.

What are you an expert at?

When customers reveal their hidden talents, they experience pride and competence, and you learn things about them that help lead them to other library resources. "I didn't know you were an expert knitter! Look at this new book on knitting we just got in! And have you heard about our knitting club, The Chronicles of Yarnia?"

What's your weirdness?

Everybody is different, and most people have at least one trait that is downright unusual. This is a great conversation starter, even among groups of friends. "I didn't know you sleepwalk!" "What do you mean, you don't like cake?"

What superpower do you want?

Answers to this question reveal a surprising amount about the ways people feel powerless or the areas in which they want to excel. Personally, we want the power to instantly absorb all the information in a Reference book simply by touching it.

Reveal your most embarrassing social media handle

Were you hobbitluvr75 on AIM in college? Was your first Instagram account snotbugmike? Tell us if you dare!

What are you most grateful for?

Research has proven that expressing gratitude enhances mood. Encourage customers to appreciate and acknowledge the good things in their life year-round, not just at Thanksgiving.

Surprisingly delightful responses to "What are you allergic to?"

I make the world a better place by . . .

When current events are getting you down, remind yourself and your community of all the good in the world by encouraging visitors to share their good works.

Are you allergic?

Pollen, pets, peanuts . . . meetings? Draw or write the thing you just can't be around. This is super helpful for accommodating your customers' needs. If the kid who always comes to programs reveals they're allergic to gluten, and you have gluten-free cookies at your next event, you've made a fan for life.

What are you most frightened of?

Invite visitors to share their fears, both rational and irrational. You'll get a lot of expected answers like snakes and spiders, but some responses signal serious stressors in people's lives that you can try to address with book displays, programming, or even just a conversation. At Andria's library, a teen wrote "my parents" in response to this prompt. As a result, staff checked in with them to see how things were going at home and made sure they knew we are caring adults they can turn to if they need any help at all.

What makes you mad?

Who doesn't need to vent from time to time? Add some Grumpy Bird art to your board to get the point across.

What's your fandom?

Everybody is a geek about something. If it's not *Star Wars* it's *Homestuck*, and if it's not *Homestuck*, it's *Hamilton*. Or maybe it's all the above! This prompt not only encourages self-definition, but it will give you valuable insight into your users interests that you can use to inform your collection development, display ideas, and programming plans.

Activity sheets

What's in your noggin?

Print a line drawing of a head and brain, with the brain part empty. Provide drawing materials so that customers can fill in what's on their mind at any given time. What's in *your* brain? (We're mostly thinking about snacks, horror novels, and how soon we can take this bra off.)

How do you feel?

This activity, often used as a therapeutic exercise, invites both introspection and creativity. Find a simple outline drawing of a person and print it along with the instruction, "Listen to your body. How does it feel?" Put out colored pencils, markers or crayons. It's fascinating to see how people represent feelings like fatigue, pain, contentment or irritation with color and shape.

If you're trying this in a children's area, look for an extremely simplified outline, even a gingerbread man shape.

Some great books to go with these expressive programs

> *Alvin Ho: Allergic to Girls, School, and Other Scary Things* by Lenore Look
> *Only You Can Be You: What Makes You Different Makes You Great* by Sally Clarkson

Same, Same But Different by Jenny Sue Kostecki-Shaw

The Things I Can Do by Jeff Mack

Itch!: Everything You Didn't Want to Know About What Makes You Scratch by Anita Sanchez

100 Things That Make Me Happy by Amy Schwartz

Layla's Happiness by Mariahadessa Ekere Tallie

I Am Peace: A Book of Mindfulness by Susan Verde

Find yourself

Part poll, part quiz, these queries require a little more setup but are fun to complete and serve as tools for self-reflection and identification.

What's your alignment?

The classic Dungeons and Dragons alignment grid of Good to Evil, Lawful to Chaotic will be familiar to some library customers but entirely new to others. We suggest priming the pump by adding well-known fictional characters as examples.

TABLE 7.3

Alignment: **Lawful Good** Example: Captain America	Alignment: **Lawful Neutral** Example: Effie Trinket	Alignment: **Lawful Evil** Example: Darth Vader
Alignment: **Neutral Good** Example: Superman	Alignment: **True Neutral** Example: Treebeard the Ent	Alignment: **Neutral Evil** Example: Voldemort
Alignment: **Chaotic Good** Example: Robin Hood	Alignment: **Chaotic Neutral** Example: Deadpool	Alignment: **Chaotic Evil** Example: Joker

Create your coat of arms

Cut a batch of shield shapes out of construction paper and load them onto your art cart or table along with markers, collage materials, and other art supplies. Print a sheet of European heraldic symbols and their meanings for inspiration.

Use Japanese heraldry for simpler set up AND a hit of cultural awareness. Japanese family crests are generally circular badges (although some are squares or other symmetrical polygons). Provide construction paper circles and print a sheet of Japanese heraldic symbols, easily discovered in a Google image search.

We love this passive program as a back-of-the-room activity for older children and adults during a fairy tale toddler storytime. Don't forget to pull a batch of books with corresponding themes.

Where's the farthest place you have traveled?

Post a world map on your board and invite customers to place a pushpin or sticker dot, or draw a circle, on their farthest-flung destination. Or use a globe that you weren't planning to do anything else with and provide dot stickers. Don't forget to mark You Are Here with a special colored sticker or lump of air-dry clay, and a length of yarn for measuring distance!

What country would you love to visit?

Same setup, different prompt. If possible, provide room for customers to write why they're interested in going.

Naturally, you're going to pair these two prompts with a display of travel guides and aspirational memoirs like *Eat, Pray, Love*.

Where is your family from?

Here's an informal, homegrown way to share what you think the results of your DNA test would show. Post a great big world map and provide sticker dots or pushpins.

Keep in mind that this can be a painful or loaded question for some—heritage and point of origin are sometimes unknown to families descended from enslaved people, refugees, or other oppressed people, who often have their identities, names, and histories suppressed or stripped from them.

Great books about family history and migration are listed below.
For kids:

A Different Pond by Thi Bui and Bao Phi
Where Are You From? by Yamile Saied Méndez
Your Name Is a Song by Jamilah Thompkins-Bigelow
A New Home by Tania de Regil
What Is a Refugee? by Elise Gravel
Inside Out and Back Again by Thanha Lai
Paper Son: The Inspiring Story of Tyrus Wong, Immigrant and Artist by
    Julie Leung
Story Boat by Kyo Maclear and Rashin Kheiriyeh
Brothers in Hope: The Story of the Lost Boys of Sudan by Mary Williams
We Are the Rope by Jacqueline Woodson

All the Way to America: The Story of a Big Italian Family and a Little Shovel by
    Dan Yaccarino
We Are Displaced: My Journey and Stories from Refugee Girls Around the World
    by Malala Yousafzai

For teens and grownups:

*Good Girls Marry Doctors: South Asian American Daughters on Obedience and
    Rebellion* by Piyali Bhattacharya
Open Borders: The Science and Ethics of Immigration by Bryan Caplan
Brother, I'm Dying by Edwidge Danticat
The Spirit Catches You and You Fall Down by Anne Fadiman
Dream Country by Shannon Gibney
Displaced: Refugee Writers on Refugee Lives by Viet Thanh Nguyen
You Bring the Distant Near by Mitali Perkins
Outcasts United: The Story of a Refugee Soccer Team That Changed a Town by
    Warren St. John
Ghana Must Go by Taiye Selasi
Here We Are: American Dreams, American Nightmares by Aarti Namdev
    Shahani
Night Sky with Exit Wounds by Ocean Vuong
The Girl Who Smiled Beads by Clemantine Wamariya
American Street by Ibi Zoboi

Height chart

How do you measure up against your favorite superhero? Are you as tall as a
bison? Where would you fit among the founding fathers (James Madison was
very, very short)? Or dinosaurs?

This passive program will literally fit on a post or even a doorframe. Spend
a fruitful hour on the Internet looking up the heights of various humans, animals, or fictional characters, then mark those heights on a sheet of roll paper
or directly on the wall (use painter's tape). Attach a ruler and a pencil with a
tether and invite customers to mark their own height.

Don't forget to tally those marks—this is a passive program that garners a
lot of interest.

Take a poem, leave a poem

You'll find lots of poetry ideas in the Poetry Month (April) section of our
chapter on A Year of Passive Programming. But poetry is a fine pursuit year-
round. A Take a Poem, Leave a Poem jar or mobile can inhabit a quiet corner

of your library waiting to dish out a little poetic inspiration whenever anyone needs it.

Find a number of short poems and print them out. Make slips to be folded, cloud shapes, banners—whatever works best for your theme and time constraints. Hang the poems from a mobile with tiny clothespins or drop them into a Big Jar. Provide blank slips, pencils, and a selection of poetry books nearby and ask customers to copy a favorite poem onto a slip and add it to the jar or mobile.

Story quilt craft

On the craft table, provide construction paper squares and display examples of what story quilt squares look like. Paper quilt squares can be decorated in a variety of ways—give teens and adults collage supplies, but you might want to limit younger customers to markers and crayons.

Encourage people to leave their story quilt squares in a basket on the table. Once you have several completed squares, line them up on a bulletin board or other vertical space. If your library has a big window, think about making quilt squares with transparency film and tissue paper or Sharpie and taping them to the window.

Books to have on hand:

The Arabic Quilt: An Immigrant Story by Aya Khalil
Sweet Clara and the Freedom Quilt by Deborah Hopkinson
Stitchin' and Pullin': A Gee's Bend Quilt by Patricia McKissack
Cassie's Word Quilt by Faith Ringgold
Show Way by Jacqueline Woodson
Dia's Story Cloth: The People's Journey of Freedom by Dia Cha

Photo contests

Now that just about everyone carries a camera in their pocket, it's relatively easy to host photo contests. They can piggyback off existing programs like photography workshops or can stand alone.

Ask customers to submit photos related to a given theme by a deadline. You might choose a unique hashtag and ask customers to post their best photos to Instagram/Twitter, or instruct them to send photo attachments to a library e-mail address using a specific subject line.

Display all entries in the library, and award prizes. We recommend you avoid ranking them in first, second, and third place. Make up silly categories based on the entries, like "best picture of a dog wearing a hat," or "best picture of a baby eating ice cream."

Stick with broad themes that are open to interpretation and inclusive. We have heard of libraries doing contests that ask customers to take a photo of their library card while they're on summer vacation, and reward whoever has traveled the farthest. While this can generate some fantastic photos of your card and customers in exotic locales, unfortunately, participation is restricted to those with the means to travel.

Here are some themes to try:

- Where I read
- A day in my life
- The world through my eyes
- Saturday afternoon
- Building a better world
- The world's best pet
- Pride
- Love (or hope, peace, friendship—abstract concepts work well)

STEAM, etcetera

All passive programs build skills: critical thinking, research, creativity, and even social skills are exercised in passive programs. They can have subtle or overt educational agendas, and you should be able to justify the specific benefits of each to administrators and staff. Here are some ideas that specifically support STEAM-based objectives.

Estimation station

A guessing jar is not only visually attractive, but great for practicing math skills. Fill your Big Jar full of candy and they'll line right up! We've also had success using LEGO pieces, crayons, balloons, or any other small items you have in bulk.

Pro tips:

- Count the items as they go in. Write the number on a slip of paper, fold it, and tape it to the underside of the jar lid—that way you won't misplace it. But if people ask—and they will—tell them you have not counted them yet, or they will try to tease the answer out of you!

- If you use candy, tape that lid closed to keep visitors from helping themselves to a treat and to ensure the number of candies remains constant. It's probably a good idea to seal the jar closed, no matter what's in it, just to be safe.
- Guesses should go in their own separate, opaque, sealed container. A plastic jug with a snap-top lid is a good option—decorate it with paint or decoupage and cut an oblong slit in the plastic lid so that entry slips can slide in. Another cute option is to use a novelty piggy bank!

Animals, animals

Animal kingdom scavenger hunt

We like animal challenges that promote awareness of the entirety of the animal kingdom, not just critters from the cute and fuzzy part. Print your scavenger hunt sheet with a list of creatures from lots of phyla. The challenge? Find a book or other material that features each type of animal. It's likely you're going to have to provide a few hints—and be sure to check that your library has a book or two on sponges if you're thinking about adding rotifera to the list.

TABLE 7.4

Common Name	Scientific Name	Sample Title
Worms	Annelida	*Worm Loves Worm* by J.J. Austrian
Spiders	Arachnida	*Diary of a Spider* by Doreen Cronin
Shellfish	Crustacea	*A House for Hermit Crab* by Eric Carle
Mollusks	Mollusca	*Escargot* by Dashka Slater
Insects	Arthropoda	*The Last Peach* by Gus Gordon
Bony fish	Osteichthyes	*This Is Not My Hat* by Jon Klassen
Sharks and rays	Chondrichthyes	*If Sharks Disappeared* by Lily Williams
Birds	Aves	*Spots in a Box* by Helen Ward
Rodents	Rodentia	*Be Quiet* by Ryan T. Higgins
Marsupials	Marsupials	*Diary of a Wombat* by Jackie French
Primates	Primates	*Orangutan Tongs* by Jon Agee

Make an easier animal scavenger hunt by printing pictures of different animals and hiding them throughout the building. The hidden benefit of a picture hunt like this is that sometimes customers spot a photo of a goliath beetle or luna moth in an unlikely spot and then find a library staff member to ask just what the heck is going on.

Or level this up by turning it into a passport program: Read Your Way through the Animal Kingdom.

Track match

Print actual-size animal footprints, number them, and mount them on your board or wall alongside a list and pictures of the animals that made them. Visitors who successfully identify all the tracks win a prize! This is a good winter program if you live in an area that gets snow, or an anytime activity for lucky libraries near the beach. Reproduce the tracks of shorebirds, crabs, dogs, and people—anyone who strolls the water's edge.

Try this with dinosaur tracks if you have the room!

Dino-match

Speaking of dinosaurs, dinosaur names are a great way to learn language connections. Make a game that challenges visitors to match the dino species name with its Latin meaning or derivation. We'll get you started.

TABLE 7.5

Extinct animal	Meaning of name
Triceratops	Three-horned face
Ornithomimus	Bird mimic
Oviraptor	Egg thief
Velociraptor	Fast thief
Tyrannosaurus rex	Tyrant lizard king
Maiosaura	Good mother lizard
Pachycephalosaurus	Thick head lizard
Pterodactyl	Wing finger
Psittacosaurus	Parrot lizard
Edmontosaurus	Lizard from Edmonton
Archaeopteryx	Ancient feather
Caudipteryx	Tail feather
Pentaceratops	Five-horned face

What's your dino name?

Also a fun way to learn Latin roots, an image search on "find your dinosaur name" will yield a variety of naming memes that put together a dinosaur name from the first letter of your name and your birth month.

Sincerely,

Postoryonyx Paula and Alamoraptor Andria

I Spy

I Spy challenges are always fun and develop focus, concentration, and observational skills. In our chapter about special spaces, we will discuss creating I Spy installations, but here are some seek-and-find games that will work anywhere.

On a board or wall

Rachel Fryd of Philadelphia Free Library inherited a giant popcorn tin full of pinback badges with her new office. She and Christopher Brown, curator of the children's literature research collection, used them to create an I Spy display on a big swath of purple velvet. Customers were challenged to find Ramona Quimby, a ladybug, a star, how many yellow pins, and so on, and the list was changed every week.

You could do this with stickers, panels from discarded comic books and graphic novels, or an art display. "Whatever you use, there just needs to be a lot of it!" says Rachel.

As an activity sheet

Even if you don't have vertical space, you can make an I Spy that comes straight out of your color printer. Take images of familiar objects and collage a whole slew of them together using graphics or photo editing software, then make a list of ten items to find.

Big Jar

If you have no space at all, you can still make an I Spy challenge with a Big Jar. Fill the jar with perler beads or something else small and slidy; then bury tiny objects inside. Customers can pick up the jar and shift it around until the buried objects are revealed. Game pieces work well in a Big Jar seek-and-find.

Write your name in cursive

Q: How do you know you're old?
A: You're old if you learned cursive in school.

Ha ha ha ugh. For better or worse, cursive is becoming a cryptic method of communication. Most young people cannot read the title of a book if it is written in cursive on the spine. Challenge them to try their hand at this mystic art. Display the cursive alphabet along with examples of how the letters actually *connect together*!

They'll gain some practice with hand-eye coordination and fine motor skills, and you'll gain an opportunity to be better at something than they are.

Invention timeline

Here's a truly fascinating look at technology, including the technology we take for granted. Which was invented first—the pocket calculator or the digital watch? Pick ten or twelve inventions and arrange them in order by date invented. Then scramble them up and challenge library users to put them in the right order. Add a level of difficulty by also listing the country where they were invented.

We'll start you off with a handy list of inventions and their time/place of origin:

TABLE 7.6

Invention	Date	Location
Paper	105 CE	China
Printing press	1450	Germany
Parachute	1470	Italy
Microscope	1590	Netherlands
Barometer	1643	Italy
Steam engine	1712	England
Hot-air balloon	1783	France
Rubber	1839	United States
Fax machine	1850	France
Elevator	1861	United States
Telephone	1876	United States
Vacuum cleaner	1901	England
Washing machine	1907	United States
Helicopter	1939	United States
Traffic signal	1923	United States

Leverage interest in inventions by showcasing a few titles about astonishing inventors:

The Day-Glo Brothers: The True Story of Bob and Joe Switzer's Bright Ideas and Brand-New Colors by Chris Barton
Whoosh!: Lonnie Johnson's Super-Soaking Stream of Inventions by Chris Barton
The Boy Who Harnessed the Wind by William Kamkwamba
Hedy Lamarr's Double Life: Hollywood Legend and Brilliant Inventor by Laurie Wallmark

The Boo-Boos That Changed the World: A True Story about an Accidental Invention by Barry Wittenstein

On a bulletin board or magnetic board

Print captioned pictures of each item. Laminate them if you can. Attach them to a magnet, a Velcro dot, or just use pushpins to attach them to the board.

Use wide tape to make a timeline, labeled with decades (or centuries!). Add a covered answer key so that players can check their answers.

As an activity sheet

List the inventions out of order alongside a timeline graphic. Players write the names of the inventions along the timeline in the order in which they think the objects were invented. Or make this a simple match game, with inventions in one column and the date of their patent in the other.

Take a fact, leave a fact

Themed Fact Challenges are great for heritage months and international holidays, but there's no reason not to keep your Fact Jar going year-round. Your customers will get used to stopping by the jar to learn a weird or fun fact every time they visit the library. Fun facts spark conversations and can lead to book recommendations and more! Books like *Ripley's Believe It or Not, IQ,* and National Geographic's *Weird but True* are helpful when you're searching for the strange and unusual.

Try these themes as sources for astounding information:

- Weird world records
- Animals
- Natural disasters
- Ancient cultures—China and the Aztecs are particularly interesting
- Medical miracles

What is it?

Shoot two pictures of familiar objects—one showing the object in its entirety and the other zoomed in on a tiny detail. Number the detailed photos and print them on a quiz sheet. This makes a great match game that exercises observation and comparison skills. Alternatively, post the numbered photos adjacent to a display of the actual objects.

Stump the librarian

Here's an anytime activity that encourages critical thinking and research skills. Make a humorous sign for your desk offering a prize to anyone who can come up with a question that desk staff can't answer. Offer an extra prize if the customer can provide the answer themselves!

Creative writing

Develop customers' literacy skills, tickle their imaginations, and help grow the next generation of authors with clever creative writing exercises.

Write a tall tale

Tall tales are fun ways to get the creative juices flowing. They don't have to make a lot of sense, and include imagination-stretching feats that necessitate the use of outrageous adjectives and sumptuous superlatives. Print sheets with a juicy leading phrase and enough space to write a short tall tale. Give your customers a wall or board to post their stories to, or a box or jar in which to drop them contest entries. Pick a winner at random and post your favorites.

SOME TALL TALE PROMPTS

- My pet can talk. And he told me. . . .
- As I was walking into the library today, I looked down and found. . . .
- My aunt invented a machine that. . . .

The neverending story/exquisite corpse

Here's a writing prompt that goes on and on, fostering creativity and sequential thought. Use your whiteboard, bulletin board, or art table to start a story. Library visitors add as much or as little as they wish but have to keep the story going.

Make your own Just-So story

How did the rat get a skinny tail? Why do crabs walk sideways? How did horses get so fast? Why are mice so small? This is a passive program that dovetails beautifully with a folktale storytime—hand it out to grownups or older children who are cooling their heels, pretending not to listen to you tell pourquoi tales. Post an example on your board or on one side of a sheet.

Art appreciation

Introduce new vocabulary, develop cultural literacy, and inspire young artists by exposing them to classic and contemporary masterpieces. Post examples of different styles of art (impressionist, cubist, surrealism, etc.). Provide descriptions of the various styles and ask participants to identify the style of each image.

Try this as a three-part match game—match an example of the artwork to a description of the style and to the style name. Some style names, like Fauvism, provide almost no clues, whereas others, like Surrealism, are easy to pick out in a crowd. Be sure the images you post are high resolution and include the name of the artist and the title of the artwork. Accompany this activity with a display of materials about art history, lives of the artists, coffee table art books, and how-to guides.

Community building

So many passive programs have a community building aspect. Book recommendation boards, writing prompts, and mobiles and garlands with art or thoughts contributed by library customers all allow people to not only see themselves in the library but also feel like they are part of a larger community of citizens and library users. The programs below are specifically geared to creating this sense of belonging and ownership.

Writing prompt

The biggest issue facing our community is . . .

The responses to this prompt give library visitors food for thought and promote inclusiveness. Not only that, but they can help your library make decisions about programming and outreach.

My wish for our community

Andria's library set up this prompt as a beautiful lobby garland. Customers wrote their wishes in permanent marker on colorful lengths of wide ribbon and tied them to a length of twine stretched along the wall.

Swap table

Many libraries are adding nonmedia items to their collections. We've heard of libraries that lend cake pans, power tools, telescopes, and even fishing rods.

Once you've started down that road, other items begin to come to mind, including less-durable or consumable items. Some libraries, especially small or rural libraries, maintain a swap table where customers can bring in items they no longer need and browse the offerings left by others. This practice can lead to misunderstandings, mess, and some truly bizarre objects being left. Keep it in check by limiting the scope of your swap table or maintaining it for a limited time.

- Yarn swaps work—provide small bins, sorted by color, fiber, or weight, for people to offload their stash and pick up new materials.
- An annual board game swap is also a great idea. Try it around the holidays as people are cleaning out their closets. Provide clear tape and markers so that corners can be mended and any missing pieces can be noted.
- Video games or DVDs are good swap items as they don't take up much space and are easily organized.
- Sports equipment and other specialty gear might work in your community. You might want to specify, "No shoes!"
- Coupon swaps are perennially popular—prime the pump with the coupon inserts from library's edition of the Sunday paper. Customers can drop off coupons for items they don't need and pick up ones for the things they do. You'll want to sift through the coupon pile every now and then and remove any that have expired.

Lead swappers into the stacks by posting booklists or call number information relevant to the swap table theme. In her book *Librarian's Guide to Passive Programming*, Emily T. Wichman recommends creating a special bookmark as a takeaway reward for customers browsing the items on offer.

No matter what you invite people to swap, make it clear with a sign that leftovers will be donated at the end of the time period or, in the case of art supplies or craft materials, may be absorbed into the library's own stash.

Little Free Library

The Little Free Library movement is a perfect example of a swap program that is limited in scope—it's just books (and maybe movies). It might seem counterintuitive for a library to keep a Little Free Library—after all, we're all Big Free Libraries—but they're visually appealing, easy to maintain, and they always look like a little treasure box. You never know what you might find in them.

We talk more about Little Free Libraries in our chapter on The Outside World. It makes sense to keep them outside the library. They're out there 24/7, reminding people that the library is looking out for them and their reading needs.

Pop culture

References to superheroes, TV shows, and other current trends engage a wide swath of the population and help dispel the myth that libraries are elite bastions of intellectual superiority out of touch with popular culture. The following all lend themselves well to writing prompts, but use your imagination to implement these ideas using the techniques described in the previous chapter.

Writing and recommendation prompts

Media tie-in

Epic series fiction adapted into movies or compulsively watchable TV with handsome guys, strong female characters, and bonus dragons are great for prompting people to read more.

Make a pop culture corner in your library especially for readers to recommend new books for fans of *Game of Thrones, Star Wars, Harry Potter,* or *The Hunger Games.* Don't stop at epic fantasy and science fiction—humor, graphic novels, and licensed characters make good prompts, too. Make sure your references are well known and current.

Here are a few clever prompts we've seen:

- What would Darth Vader read?
- You read nothing, Jon Snow!
- The Restricted Section: What should a Harry Potter fan read next?
- Phunny Phiction for Phans of Phineas and Ferb
- Dora Stories: Recommend a book for kids who like to explore
- Stranger Books: Weird sci-fi for fans of the up-side down

If you watch that, read this

Draw a chart on your board, fill in the first few lines as examples, and challenge visitors to make their own connections between TV shows and books. Here are a few examples for kids, teens, and grownups to get things started.

Recommendation prompts get customers to contribute to your reader advisory repertoire.

TABLE 7.7

If you watch that...	...read this
Gravity Falls	*Eerie Elementary* by Jack Chabert
Thomas the Tank Engine	*Locomotive* by Brian Floca
Schitt's Creek	*Furiously Happy* by Jenny Lawson
Veep	*Fleishman is in Trouble* by Taffy Brodesser-Akner
Spongebob Squarepants	*Captain Underpants* by Dav Pilkey

Additional prompts to try

- Sounds good: What are you listening to?
- What TV show are you binging right now?
- Who would you cast in the film version of....?
- What book should be made into a movie?
- What celebrity do you want to meet and why?
- What's the best movie you've seen this year?

Opinion polls

Vote for your favorite . . .

Options might include Disney princess, superhero, Star Wars droid, and so on. Every fandom has its subfandoms—find out where your customers' loyalties lie.

Villain cage match!

Who would win, Voldemort or Venom? Thanos or Maleficent? At Andria's library, this is a popular activity at Anime Nights and has sparked many in-depth conversations and debates among teen participants. They'll even opt to continue discussing hypothetical death matches between favorite anime characters instead of watching a second episode at the event.

Book or movie—which was better?

List books like *The Hunger Games, Harry Potter, The Shining, If Beale Street Could Talk, Outlander, Diary of a Wimpy Kid*, and so on, depending on the ages and interests of your library customers and whatever is currently popular. Every time Paula has put up this poll, at least one person has expressed their very strong opinion by adding as many tick marks as will fit in the voting area.

What movie should we show next?

We've tried this as an open-ended prompt and never achieved satisfactory results. Framing it as a poll with a limited number of options means that there will at least be a majority opinion at the end of the day.

Activity sheets

Why'd they wear that?

Make a match game out of fashion items with odd names—mules, fascinator, gaiter, houppelande, wimple, unitard. Use the very entertaining book *Why'd They Wear That?* by Sarah Albee as a source.

Manga match game

Challenge participants to match the character with the book or signature item with character. Incorporate images from the books for an extra shot of visual literacy development.

Magical creatures match game

Most cultures have benign or harmful spirits as part of their mythology. Pair pictures of fairies from around the world with the culture they come from.

TABLE 7.8

Supernatural creature	Country or culture of origin
Tien	Vietnam
Patupaiarehe	Maori
Sidhe	Ireland
Mogwai	China
Jogah	Iroquois
Douen	Caribbean
Kitsune	Japan
Aziza	Dahomey
Chaneque	Mexico

Make a healthy choice

Rank snacks, candy, or fast food favorites in order by calories, grams of fat (or sugar). Use the manufacturers' info and let the kids know they can find these exact numbers online.

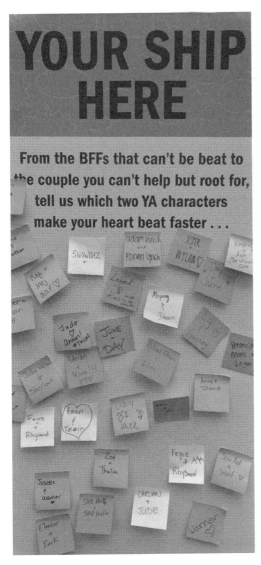

OTPs and BFFs at Book Expo.

Create your own dialogue

Photocopy comic strips, or pages from graphic novels, and white out the text in the speech bubbles. Participants write in dialogue to fit the images.

I ship it!

The rise of fan fiction redefined the word "shipping" to mean imagining romantic relationships that don't exist in the original narrative, or between characters from two separate stories or universes. Passive programs based on this concept encourage creative thinking and even empathy, as one must be able to understand the characters' feelings and motivations before playing matchmaker.

Read "The Sweet Science of Shipping" by Maggie Owens on fandom.com for an entertaining and informative quick education—and if you don't mind coming away with the image of Sonic the Hedgehog pregnant with Shrek's baby seared onto your brain.

Speaking of fan fiction: your customers, especially teens, are probably already writing it. Why not encourage and support them by hosting a fan fiction contest or writing group, in addition to one of these ideas?

On a board or wall

Provide post-Its or heart shapes for customers to write the fictional pairing they'd love to see: Aragorn and Tonks? Loki and Kamala Khan?

In a Big Jar

Print names of characters (and their provenance) on slips. Customers pull two names and decide whether this couple would be platonic, romantic, a OTP (One True Pairing), a Crack Pairing (totally crazy but just might work), Enemies, or something else. Naturally, they should also come up with the couple's Ship Name. Andria's library has found this to be an excellent icebreaker activity at teen advisory board meetings.

Use a website like knowyourmeme.com to educate yourself on pop culture relationship terminology (if necessary).

Write your name

There are several pop culture franchises with their own alphabet. Add value to movie screenings and other staff-led programs related to these universes by printing a copy of the alphabet and challenging participants to write their name in Klingon, Dothraki, Aurebesh (Star Wars), or Wakandan.

Seriously silly

Here are a few passive programs that don't have anything to do with anything—they're just fun. Roll out any of these any time your department needs a shot of unexpected whimsy.

Megan Emery Shadlich's Random Table of Who Knows What

In her book *Cooking Up Library Programs Teens and 'Tweens Will Love*, Ms. Shadlich recommends this method of making the most out of stray objects and supplies. "This is where you'll put out your random toys to be played with until they die (even if that's just a few days) . . . the donation of 10,000 foam stars (learn to make constellation mobiles!), and so on. . . ." We love letting your library customers lead the way—they'll show YOU what to do with that box of old ribbon someone donated.

Keep an eye on this table of random stuff, though, and don't let it start to look junky. We're no fans of pristine library spaces, but a mess is not inviting, and it makes the library look like an uncared-for place.

Jigsaw jar

Fill a jar with pieces from a jigsaw puzzle. Make sure most pieces have the printed sides facing out. Customers try to guess what the completed image is. It probably goes without saying—but we're going to say it anyway—pick a puzzle with a simple image. Kittens in a basket or a picture of a superhero won't be too hard, but a puzzle featuring, say, the castles of Lichtenstein would be nearly impossible.

Chimerical creatures

The chimera was a mythological creature with a lion's head, a goat's body, and a snake's tail. Make up your own chimerical creature and draw it!

This or that polls

Taking inspiration from the famous "this or that?" icebreaker, pop one of these polls up on your whiteboard, bulletin board, or voting jars whenever there's a lull in the passive program action. Or keep two paper chains going—every link a visitor adds is a vote. These are the most fun when you keep the subject matter light and stay away from truly controversial topics!

Here are some ideas to get you started:

M&Ms or Skittles?
Sneakers or boots?
Netflix or Hulu?
Basketball or football?
Apples or oranges?
Starburst or Jolly
    Ranchers?
PlayStation or Xbox?
Coke or Pepsi?
Cake or Pie?

INSTANT REPLAY:

A teen girl turns in her Monday Maze worksheet with a sheepish expression.

Her: "I messed up a bunch of times before I figured it out."

Me: "it's ok, these mazes are like life - it doesn't matter how many wrong turns you take, as long as you end up in the right place."

Her: "whoa"

Me: "you didn't know the maze was also a metaphor, did you?"

8

If You Build It, They Will Come: Special Spaces for Passive Programs

The point of this book so far has been to prove that passive programming is adaptable to any library, regardless of the space or resources available. We stand by that statement. We know that in many libraries, extra space can be as scarce as extra funding.

However, if you can manage to carve out a special spot—a corner, a nook, or a bench—it opens up an additional world of passive programming possibilities. Look at your area with fresh eyes: are there any spaces that can be repurposed? Can you rearrange furniture in a creative way? Can you dismantle that display that never gets any love and turn it into a listening or sensory station?

In this chapter, we'll look at some methods for using special spaces to offer unique passive programs that meet developmental and behavioral needs, foster different kinds of learning, and engage customers in unexpected ways. Most of these spaces work best as a long-term or permanent feature with a variety of rotating activities, because you want customers to develop the habit of using the space and checking to see what's new in it, every time they come to the library.

Sensory station

A sensory station is a fantastic addition to the children's department of the library because little kids discover and learn about their world by touching, smelling, and tasting things and developing the skills to describe them. Sensory stations give them opportunities to sharpen their senses and practice articulating their reactions.

Don't rule out sensory programs for teens and adults, either. Teens will be extremely enthusiastic about taste tests in particular because they love to eat and to voice their opinions, and because their experiences and vocabulary are broader than those of children, you'll get thoughtful and hilarious responses. Even a smelling station could be adapted for adults—since our sense of smell is so deeply connected to our memories, you could prompt visitors to fill in the blank: "when I smell this I think of _____."

The best location for a sensory station is an out-of-the-way nook or corner that is quiet enough for the explorer to concentrate on what they are feeling or smelling, but not so hidden that customers will overlook it. Ideally you will use a shelf, windowsill, table, or A/V cart to set up a station, but with a bit of ingenuity, you can even implement some of these ideas on a vertical space or a corner of your service desk.

Depending on your library community, you may want to set up your sensory station along a visible sightline so you can monitor it closely, but regardless, this area should be checked a few times a day to ensure your materials are stocked and neatly arranged.

Load a nearby shelf or display with books on the senses such as those listed below, or titles that are thematically linked to the specific activity.

Touch and Feel books:

My five senses by Aliki
My Three Best Friends and Me, Zulay by Cari Best
Six Dots: A Story of Young Louis Braille by Jen Bryant
The Black Book of Colors by Menena Cottin
Silent Days, Silent Dreams by Allen Say

Blind boxes

What do your fingers tell you? Can you identify an object without seeing it? These types of interactive exhibits are common (and hugely popular) in science museums and can easily be recreated in your library. Set up one at a time, or make several and set them all on a shelf.

Some interesting objects to try: fruits and vegetables (great tie-in with a cooking program), hand tools, art supplies, natural objects like pine cones and seashells, sports balls of various types, kitchen utensils, or a variety of stuffed animals.

A variation on this to try with older children and teens is to write a message, using a ballpoint pen or stylus on the inside of the box, pressing down hard to indent your strokes into the cardboard. Challenge your visitors to read the message using only their fingertips. Try this with Braille, too, next to a poster of the Braille alphabet.

Create an easy blind box

1. Find a clean, sturdy container of appropriate size for each object. Shoeboxes work well for small hands, but you may want a bigger box for teens or adults.
2. Cut a hole in the box. It should be big enough to reach one hand in and feel the object, but smaller than the object itself. You don't want people to pull the object out of the box through the hole.
3. Put the object in the box. If you are using a small object like a seashell or other item that fits in the palm of your hand, consider gluing it to the bottom of the box so it can't be removed. Use glue to seal the box closed.
4. Post a sign on the outside of the box or next to it, challenging library visitors to reach in and guess the contents.
5. Provide hints by displaying books and other library materials that relate to the mystery object nearby.

If you don't have an available shelf or table, you can implement this concept on a bulletin board or other vertical space by gluing samples of various flat materials (bark, velvet, sponge, carpet, window screen, sandpaper) to numbered squares of cardboard. Engineer a flap to hide the samples from view.

Smelling zoo

What does your nose know? This sensory exercise will supplement any number of staff-led programs. Collect spices to go along with a cultural or cooking program or aromatic plants to accompany a garden program. Place a sample of each odorous item in a small "sniff box" and number the boxes. Participants smell each box and attempt to identify the odors.

This works great as a matching game: list all the odorous objects on an answer sheet and challenge people to write the number of the box containing each listed item.

Level up this activity and help young people develop verbal literacy skills by providing space on the answer sheets for describing the scents. This is an excellent mental exercise that provides real-world practice with adjectives and associations.

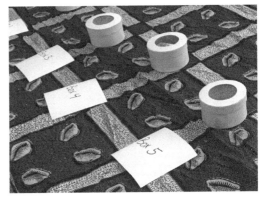

Make or buy small boxes with mesh windows in the lids to make a Smelling Zoo.

Your smelling zoo can live in your sensory station with instructions in a sign holder. Or make it portable by hot gluing your smelling boxes to a sheet of foam core board (just make sure the boxes are spaced far enough from each other that the scents don't intermingle).

Pro tip: A smelling zoo is an unexpected addition to the library's table at outreach events! You can leverage interest in the smells into a conversation about the variety of programs that can be found at the library.

Create an easy sniff box

1. Collect small cardboard gift boxes, sturdy enough to withstand handling.
2. Take off the lids. Use a craft knife to cut a hole in each lid, no larger than 2"×2".
3. Glue a piece of net, tulle, or a scrap of cut-up pantyhose to the inside of each lid, securely covering the hole.
4. Put your smell sample in the box and replace the lid. Secure the lid with hot glue.

Alternatively, leave the lid off and hot glue a square of your chosen material to cover the entire top of the box. If you choose this method, be sure that your material is opaque enough that the smelly item can't be identified visually.

Note: Sniff boxes can't be reused. The odor of the previous sample will linger. If you've got your supplies out, you might as well make a big batch of these boxes, so your next smelling zoo will be ready to be loaded with new samples once the first set loses their potency.

Spices of the world

Pair a set of sniff boxes featuring herbs and spices from around the world with a map and a match game to increase cultural awareness. The challenge is to match the numbered box with the name of the spice and its country of origin and then to locate that country on the map.

Some good spices for this program are saffron (Greece), clove (Indonesia), cinnamon (Sri Lanka), sage (Mexico and American Southwest), basil (India), and star anise (China).

Holiday cookie match

Load your boxes with cinnamon, vanilla, peanut butter, and ginger. Smellers identify the substances, or match them to the cookies they are featured in: rugelach, sugar cookie, peanut butter cookies, and gingersnaps. We're not saying you absolutely have to give out cookies as prizes for correct guesses, but it would be pretty sweet if you did.

Essential oils

Various essential oils are said to produce feelings of calm or relaxation, or to provide a hit of energy. Put a few drops of oil onto cotton balls and pop them in your boxes. Challenge customers match the smell to the name of the oil, and provide space on your answer sheet for them to describe how the scent makes them feel. Then give them a list of the properties each oil claims to have, so they can compare their impressions to the claims.

A few easily identified oils for your smelling zoo are peppermint, lemon, lavender, eucalyptus, basil, and chamomile.

What's on your hotdog?

Easy and silly, this is a simple match game that can be put together in a flash with items from your refrigerator. Use ketchup, mustard, Sriracha, onions, and relish. Keep these condiments from soaking through the boxes by lining the bottoms with plastic wrap.

Smells Like School Spirit

Supplement your back-to-school programming with a smelling station featuring scents of nonedible objects associated with school: crayons, pencil shavings, hand sanitizer, magic markers, dirty gym socks(?!)

More ideas

Don't stop with these suggestions—any dried spices and essential oils are ideal for a smelling zoo program. You can also try various condiments, extracts, and sauces. Try vinegar, hot sauce, fish sauce, or soy sauce.

And don't forget nonedible items. Smelling the difference between various cleaning solutions sounds like an excellent challenge (and one that is sure to stymie most kids)! Apply liquids to a cotton ball or piece of paper towel and pop them in the box. It should go without saying, but you'll want to stick with things like laundry detergent, glass cleaner, and lemon-scented furniture polish—stay away from ammonia, bleach, and other toxic chemicals.

Taste tests

Can you taste the difference? How sophisticated is your palate? Comparing different brands or flavors is an activity with wide appeal. Put out numbered samples and provide rating sheets with space for not only evaluating each sample's appeal but also using descriptive language to describe the taste. Or make it a match game, with each flavor or brand listed on an answer sheet.

If you have a whiteboard, chalkboard, or bulletin board, make a grid for taste testers to enter their guesses. Tip: skinny washi tape is a quick and attractive way to make straight lines on a board.

Caveat: Anything involving food may be best undertaken in dedicated program areas, depending on your library's policy regarding eating in the library. Place a big trash can next to your sample table—and don't leave this unmonitored. Be aware of any potential allergens contained in your samples in case customers ask, and consider posting allergen information.

Provide an answer sheet, let testers vote for their favorite and least favorite flavors, or make a grid on a board with lots of space for tasters to record their guesses and—most importantly—reactions. Challenge customers to stretch past using "weird" as their only description by providing examples of taste adjectives, asking about flavor associations, or asking for made-up words. Those Chicken and Waffles Lays, for example, are "doughigreasilous."

Take the Pepsi challenge

This one is best for grownups or teens. Number a set of tiny cups from 1 through 4. Pour small amounts of Pepsi, Coke, Diet Coke, and your local store brand cola in each cup—make sure all the Coke goes in the 1 cups, and all the Pepsi goes in the 2's, and so on. Set them on a table in rows.

TABLE 8.1

Name	Pepsi	Coke	Diet Coke	RC Cola
Andria	4	2	3	1
Paula	4	3	2	1
Jessica	4	2	3	1

What kinds of maniacs work at Lays?

Buy bags of potato chips in unusual flavors—you may have a local brand like Route 66, Zapp's, or Utz, but Lays are available nationwide and often come out with some truly strange chip flavors. Chicken and Waffles potato chips? Yikes. We strongly suspect some of these were invented for the sole purpose of feeding them to unsuspecting subjects and watching their reactions. Set them out in numbered bowls on a table and let the fun begin. Don't forget napkins!

More ideas

Pop Tarts (cut them into pieces), jelly beans, and those fancy flavors of Oreos are also terrific taste test candidates. Or try using salsa, hummus, and various dips, or assorted flavors of yogurt or pudding. Use tiny condiment cups and taster spoons—available at restaurant supply stores or online—to set out small samples for tasting.

Listening station

We all know that some people are visual learners and some are auditory. A listening station meets the needs of your auditory learners and can be adapted in a variety of ways for different activities and users of all ages.

One centrally located listening station in your library could have an iPod or MP3 player loaded with tracks labeled for Children, Teens, and Adults, and activity sheets and/or displays that correspond to each.

Or, make a listening station one part of your overall sensory station. In libraries where space is tight, all you really need is a shelf with space for a device and a hook to hang the headphones on.

If your library maintains a collection of Vox books or other talking books for children, your listening station is halfway there! Shelve this collection in a place where you can park a mini armchair and provide a sweet pair of child-size headphones (and a box of wipes).

In the very best of circumstances, you may have access to or have the ability to purchase a purpose-built listening chair. Kids will undoubtedly use these to plug in their phones and listen to their own music, but you can also provide preloaded podcasts or e-audiobooks that connect with your Summer Reading theme or other programs.

Setup

- Provide a comfy chair so listeners can settle in and relax.
- Decide if you're going to enforce time limits (and if so, how) or not.
- Keep your components from walking away. Use outdated devices like a CD player, an iPod or MP3 player, and consider using zip ties or even superglue to secure your device.

Earbuds and headphones

Many adults and teens have their own earbuds or headphones—but don't assume that this is the case. Provide a pair of headphones (and antibacterial wipes!) secured to your listening station. If your headphones keep walking away, keep them at the desk and post a sign at the station with directions to sign out headphones from a staff member.

As a last resort, perhaps your library can be convinced to sell earbuds or cheap headphones at an extremely nominal price.

Audiobooks

Load a new set of titles each week. A young child can listen to a story any time they're in the library. A struggling reader can listen and follow along with the book at the same time and improve their literacy. Adults and teens can sample a new book, then borrow it from the library on CD, Playaway, or as a digital download if they like it. Short story or humorous essay collections on audio are great for listening stations, too.

Display text and audio copies of the featured titles, along with any flyers or pamphlets you have about Overdrive/Libby, Hoopla, or other digital download services.

Content suggestions: Short subjects for drop-in listening

Best American Short Stories
Best American Science Writing
Selected Shorts

Poetry

There is nothing like listening to a poem read in the poet's own voice. Every tone and inflection, every rhythm and cadence, is exactly as it was intended for optimal appreciation and understanding. Take your Poetry month programming to the next level by filling your listening station with recordings of poets reading their work. Of course, you will display collections of the featured poets' work nearby.

Make it interactive

- Create a worksheet with the name of each poem and space for people to describe how the poem made them feel.
- Provide paper for customers to compose their own poem, and a mobile, garland, or "Poet-tree" to hang it on.
- Post a whiteboard or a stack of sticky notes near the listening station so that listeners can write and share their reactions.

Content suggestions

Search online at thepoetryarchive.org for beautiful recordings of Walt Whitman, Billy Collins, Langston Hughes, Gwendolyn Brooks, John Berryman, and more. Library of Congress also has a large online archive of Poetry Audio Recordings. Survey your audiobook collection for Elizabeth Acevedo, Jacqueline Woodson, Maya Angelou, and more.

Mine your children's poetry section for books with CDs (remember CDs?). These seldom-used resources may be in pristine condition and deserve a listen or two before being consigned to obsolescence.

Hip Hop Speaks to Children
Poetry Speaks to Children
Peter Yarrow songbooks
The Carnival of the Animals by Jack Prelutsky

Podcasts

Are you a podcast person? If you're not, someone on your staff surely is. Local history and true crime are always popular, but podcasts can also be excellent ways to introduce your customers to voices and stories they may not hear in their daily life. Load your listening station with timely podcasts that correspond to the season, current events, or library programs. Look for short podcasts—not many people come to the library in order to sit for an hour or more listening to Earwolf.

Make it interactive

Park a little whiteboard nearby so that listeners can suggest their favorite podcasts or comment on what they've heard.

Content suggestions: Program tie-ins

- Hosting an author visit? Find their podcast interviews.
- Showing a movie? Play the podcast reviews.
- General interest: "Merriam-Webster's Word of the Day," "The Way I Heard It by Mike Rowe," or "Retropod"
- Science: "Scientific American's 60-Second Science"
- Immigration: "Que Pasa Midwest"
- Economics: "The Indicator"
- Crime: "Criminal"
- Foreign language: The "News in Slow Spanish (or French or German)" from Linguistica360

Note: check the podcast descriptions to make sure the language is PG-13 if your listening station will be frequented by younger listeners.

Speeches

Augment your history and heritage month programs with live recordings of famous speeches. Hearing these speeches delivered with the passion and intensity intended by their authors makes them easier to understand and brings history to life.

Make it interactive

Create a worksheet for listeners to match the speech to the speaker or the historic event at which they spoke.

Park a whiteboard by the listening station with a writing prompt: How does President Obama's speech make you feel? What does Greta Thunberg make you want to do?

Content suggestions: Great speeches on YouTube

"I have a Dream"—Martin Luther King Jr.
"The Gettysburg Address"—Abraham Lincoln
"We Chose to Go to the Moon"—John F. Kennedy
"A Day Which Will Live in Infamy"—Franklin D. Roosevelt
"You are Stealing Our Future"—Greta Thunberg
"A More Perfect Union"—Barack Obama

Multicultural music

Load your listening station with music from different cultures to supplement heritage month programs or to celebrate holidays such as Passover, Christmas, or Eid.

Make it interactive

Offer a word search made from song titles or lyrics.

Make a match game with the types of instruments used and their names.

Set out art supplies and a prompt to draw a picture of images or feelings that the music invokes for the listener.

Content suggestions

Search terms for finding pop or traditional music from around the world. These include musical styles and names of traditional instruments.

- Africa: highlife, Afrobeat
- Central Africa: Soukous
- South Africa: kwaito
- China: C-pop
- Korea: K-pop
- Japan: J-pop, koto
- India: bhangra, raga, sitar
- Indonesia: Indo pop, gamelan
- Philippines: OPM
- Caribbean: reggae, ska, compas
- Mexico and Central America: salsa, bachata
- Portugal: fado
- Cuba: reggaeton

Chill zone

Libraries are no longer the hushed hallowed halls of yore—and while we love our noisy, energetic spaces, sometimes folks big and small crave a quiet corner.

Many schools have discovered the magic of a tucked-away comfy space for reading or reflection without distraction, and we've been seeing more of them in libraries too. A diffuser, ambient noise machine, or a burbling fish tank can help mask outside noises and promote peace.

Kids soaking up the latest *Dog Man* or *Nathan Hale's Hazardous Tales* will seek out a secluded spot. Teens like a nook with natural noise canceling so that they can concentrate on their music, and adults appreciate the peace that accompanies limited or gentle sensory input. People of all ages with autism may need a refuge from sensory stimulation, especially when the rest of the library is booming with activity.

Stock your chill zone with materials and resources on mindfulness and stress reduction. Quiet moments are ideal for taking stock, listening to your body, and supplying what it needs. Customers (and staff!) may seek out your spot so that they can concentrate, but they leave it with a heightened sense of well-being.

An awkward or out-of-the-way nook makes a great Chill Zone.

Setup

You don't need everything on this list, but items like these will help create a soothing environment and foster self-care. Friends, relatives, and coworkers may have some of these items lying around unused at home and be willing to donate them.

- Signage clearly designating it as a chill zone
- Comfy chair or yoga mat
- Essential oil diffuser
- Lavender eye pillow
- Wind chimes and a tiny fan to make them tinkle
- Ambient music or noise machine
- Filtered lighting
- Paint-with-water drawing board such as a Buddha Board
- Fish tank
- Poster of yoga poses or qi gong diagrams and instructions
- Posters of peaceful landscapes: empty beaches, mountains, forests, sunrises, and so on.

Suggestions for chill zone activities

- Coloring sheets, especially abstract patterns like mandalas
- Information about meditation and yoga apps (for kids: Moovlee)
- Even better, a library tablet preloaded with these apps
- Printouts of meditation instructions, breathing exercises, and affirmations to take home (Body Scan Meditation is a good one for kids: imagine a butterfly landing on your feet, knees, tummy, etc.)

Change up your chill zone to correspond with the seasons or heritage months: for Black History Month, play a recording of Maya Angelou reading *On the Pulse of Morning*; for Asian Heritage Month, gamelan music and ragas. In December, find resources for combating holiday stress.

And of course, you'll set up a display of books about self-care and relieving stress.

Books for inspiration

My Magic Breath by Alison Taylor and Nick Ortner
Here and Now by Julia Denos
Pearl by Molly Idle
A Stone Sat Still by Brendan Wenzel

This Book of Mine by Sarah Stewart
Journey, Quest, Return by Aaron Becker

Active zone or circuit challenge

The flip side of the chill zone is the active zone! Woo! Physical activity is another means of reducing stress, but most importantly, it's a developmental need of all children and young adults and is crucial to their health and wellness. After sitting still and listening all day in school, kids are full of pent-up energy. Without a healthy way to release it, they may find it difficult to focus on homework, follow instructions, or avoid disruptive behavior.

Consider setting up an active zone in your children's or teen space. You'll give your young people a place to "shake their wiggles out" and develop their balance, coordination, and motor skills by completing physical challenges. Don't forget to switch up the activities on a regular basis.

Not everybody has the space to host a daily dance party. One way to help people burn off extra energy when you don't have much space is to create a circuit challenge. Just like a circuit-training course in a park or gym, you can make signs suggesting physical feats and post them around the library.

Run in place while you sing the alphabet song! Touch your toes ten times! Proceed to the next sign on tiptoe! Stamp your hand or punch your card at each station and take it to the desk when you're done for a prize!

Active zone

Setup

- A space large enough for kids to move and jump around without hurting themselves or others
- Posters and signage clearly designating it as an active zone
- A whiteboard or bulletin board where you can post the activity of the day (or week)

Suggested activities

- Mini dance party: set a timer for 3 minutes and dance until it dings
- Jumping jacks or other calisthenics
- Can you plank?
- Stand on one foot for as long as possible
- STRRRRRRETCH for 30 seconds
- Simple yoga poses
- Run in place until the timer dings

- Rub your tummy while patting your head
- Walk like a penguin to the wall and back
- Do as many pushups as you can

Circuit challenge

Setup

Find spots in your library that will accommodate limited physical activity without getting in the way of other customers or staff.

Write and print instructions (remember, no handwritten signs!) for each station and mount them on foam core board or place in sign holders. You can also use stickers on the floor, banners hanging from the ceiling, or any other visual cues you devise to help visitors locate each station.

Decide if and how participants will track their progress through the stations. You can leave a supply of cards at the first station and attach a self-inking stamp or a hole punch to each subsequent station. Stickers are also an option. Since you are relying on the honor system, you may be tempted to skip this whole rigamarole, but your library athletes will gain pride, confidence, and a sense of competence from completing their training cards.

"Dance for as long as it takes you to sing Twinkle Twinkle Little Star" works just fine as a timing device, but it can be fun to add an oversized egg timer or a timer from a defunct board game to your circuit stations as well.

Suggested activities

See all the activities above under Active Zone, but also:

- Be the animal: waddle like a penguin, hop like a bunny, stalk like a tiger, crawl like a crab, etc.
- Take giant steps, walk on tiptoe, or take baby steps to the next station.
- Library safari: at each stop make a different animal noise.
- Be the books—use one book with lots of movement to create a combination story walk/active circuit, or feature a different book (with related action) at each station.

Book inspirations

How do you Wokka-Wokka by Elizabeth Bleumle
How do you dance by Thyra Heder
Wiggle by Doreen Cronin
Going on a Bear Hunt by Helen Oxenbury
How to Two by David Soman

Buddy bench

Here's another idea borrowed from schools. A buddy bench is a spot where a kid can sit to signal "I am feeling shy" or "I am looking to make a friend." This is not as much an activity as it is an exercise in fostering self-awareness, empathy, and compassion, but the world can always use more of all those things.

Naturally, a buddy bench is only appropriate in the children's section, unless maybe your library is hosting a singles' night? And even then, no.

Setup

- Bench
- Signage: Looking for a friend? Feeling shy?
- Puzzles or toys that encourage cooperative action
- Display books and movies about friendship

Make it interactive

- The Friendship Chain: when a shy child makes a new friend at the Buddy Bench, they can both put their names on strips of paper that get added to a paper chain.
- Friends Hang Out Together: same as above, but names are written on precut shapes that hang from a mobile or garland.
- Friendship Rocks! If your library has a painted rock garden (see our chapter on the outside world for more details) new friends can paint a rock together and find a special place to plant it.

Book inspiration

The Buddy Bench by Patty Brozo

I Spy

We touched on these visually engaging activities that build focus, concentration, and attention to detail in the previous chapter, but here's how to do it on a bigger scale in a special space.

If you have room, you can create a walk-in I Spy installation—we've seen library nooks packed floor to ceiling with odd and interesting objects. Follow the same set up instructions described below, but use the walls and ceiling of your nook.

If you don't have that much room or that many objects, set up your I Spy challenge in a display case—easy to see into, hard for little hands to mess with.

Change out the whole thing periodically to reflect seasonal themes. If no display case is on offer, ask around for an unused aquarium or pet cage.

Survey your surroundings for items to use. Survey your coworkers, too. You never know who has a collection of Hot Wheels cars or Star Wars action figures at home and is willing to let you put them in a display case with a checklist, until you ask.

Think creatively when you peer into your closets and storage spaces. When you do your periodic purge of the toy cupboard or Lost and Found box, be on the lookout for small, colorful items that might work in an I Spy challenge.

Take inspiration from the professionals and choose a theme. A completely random collection of objects without a unifying color, material, or subject just looks like a pile of junk.

Pro tip: one shortcut to creating an I Spy display with a unified color scheme is to assemble all the objects you want to use and spray paint them all the same color!

Needless to say, you'll display your I Spy books right next to this fun passive program.

Setup

- Select a display case or other space to dedicate to I Spy.
- Line your case or cover walls with plain or patterned paper that sets the color palette or theme for the display.
- Pick your objects. Pick unusual items in lots of different sizes.
- If creating an image-based checklist, photograph each item before placing it in the assemblage. If a coworker is loaning their prized collection for the display, create a photo inventory of all items as soon as you receive them.
- Hang items from the top and sides of the case, and from the shelves to create lots of visual interest.
- Create challenge sheets—if prereaders will be taking your challenge, be sure the checklist shows the picture of each item to be found. Either create checklists of certain items for people to find or ask them to list as many items as they can find in five minutes.
- Don't forget a sign!

Suggestions

- Animal toys and figures
- Superhero toys and insignia
- Toys and other items with a Star Wars/Harry Potter/other theme
- Hand tools
- Kitchen utensils
- Sports equipment

- Plastic fruits, vegetables, and other food
- Game pieces—this is a great final use for games that have lost critical pieces. If you do this in a display case, make color copies of the game boards and use them as background.

Photo booth

Give your customers every chance to document their visit to the library. Their pictures will become part of their own memories, establishing the library as a fun, engaging place, and prompting return visits. And if they share their photos with friends or on social media, even better—that's free advertising (word-of-mouth, the best kind) for your library and programs!

Still life project studio

A tiny light box photo studio is a great addition to a craft table. Not only do your customers get to record their creation at its best and before it gets crushed in their backpack on the way home, but hopefully they will also post their picture to social media. Don't forget to put your library's hashtag or Instagram ID on the photo frame, and to count photo booth usage stats as a separate number from your craft table stats!

Due to the rise of eBay and Etsy, there are plenty of light boxes available to buy online at a variety of price points. Or, if you have a friendly graphics department, they may be persuaded to make a professional version of a photo box printed with your library's logo and hashtag.

If you're very crafty, you can even make one yourself.

Don't miss an opportunity to promote your library — if you make a beautiful photo op prop like this, be sure to add the library's logo and hashtag.

Setup

1. Cover a box or a rectangle of packing foam with attractive paper to use as a pedestal.
2. Find a box to use as your booth. It should be larger than a shoebox but not so large as to be unwieldy. The box a case of wine comes in is just about right.
3. Spray paint the inside of the large box white. Allow to dry.
4. Cut the top out of the box out to provide light from above.
5. Cut most of the side panels out and tape translucent white paper over the openings. Tissue paper is a bit delicate but it will do. Frosted contact paper is an option.
6. Cut an inverted U shape from the front of the box and fold it toward you flat on the table. Be sure to leave an inch or so on three sides to make a frame for the picture.
7. Cut a piece of white poster board the width of your box and about twice as deep. Wedge this between the bottom front of the box and the top back so that it curves.
8. Paint the outside of the box. Print your library's logo and hashtag and add these to the frame on the front.

Stop motion animation studio

Use a library tablet loaded with animation software—or just use Apple's onboard time-lapse setting—to make stop motion animation projects. It's a lot easier than it sounds to create a mini studio for amateur auteurs.

Setup

As with the photo booth project above, you'll need a box to serve as backdrop and frame. A large-ish box works best—bigger than a shoebox but small enough to fit your space.

1. Cut most of the top of the box out to provide light from above.
2. Cut the side panels at the top, bottom, and front, so that both sides can swing toward the back. This will make it easier to manipulate objects.
3. Cut an inverted U shape from the front of the box and fold it down to make a stage.
4. Provide paper in a variety of colors that customers can decorate to create custom backdrops.
5. Add a stand for the tablet or phone. Purchase a small tripod or clamp, or you can make one from a toilet paper tube and pushpins.

Post a list of animation apps people can download to their own devices, and consider adding signage clearly stating that the animation studio is for independent use, and advertise the date and time of your next animation workshop.

Selfie station—Instagram-ready!

What are you doing in the library today? What are you working on?

These make great prompts for a whiteboard or chalkboard selfie station. Write the question at the top of the board and provide markers for customers to write their answer. Don't forget the library logo and hashtag. Or post the question on a bulletin board or wall and provide a tiny whiteboard for inscribing answers.

A quick and easy prompt is "What are you checking out today?" Take a selfie with the book, movie, game, or cake pan you found at the library, and don't forget to tag us on Instagram! Circulation staff often misses out on the delightful customer interactions that are programming librarians' bread and butter, and setting up a selfie station near checkout gives them a chance to share in the fun and engage with library users in a new way. Also: free advertising!

Ask a question that relates to the theme of your storytime, lecture, performance or book club, and you've added a passive program that supplements an active program, doubles your participation stats, and gives your customers a tangible way to remember the event.

Nature nooks

Create a space in your library for nature and wildlife appreciation. There's likely no shortage of materials in your collection that you can pull to display in these spaces. Many customers—especially the young ones—who enjoy watching the birds or the frogs will naturally want to learn more about them and those books will fly out the door.

Birdwatching

If you are fortunate enough to have windows that look onto a natural setting, place a bird feeder within view of the window. Print an identification guide that includes the birds that are likely to visit and post it next to the window. Once these are in place, there are a number of ways to leverage your bird feeder into passive programming.

Observation log

Make an observation log so that your customers can contribute their bird sightings. Include date, time of day, species, weather, and what they saw the bird doing—perching, singing, eating, and interacting with other birds.

Library life list

Create a takeaway checklist or card of the birds in your identification guide so customers can keep their own record of the birds they've spotted.

Observation illustration

Set out paper and art supplies near your nature observatory, along with a sign suggesting that visitors draw the birds they see at the feeder. Supplement this passive program with books on nature illustration.

Library pet

No birdies outside your window? Consider a quiet, contained pet such as a fish, turtle, frog or even a tarantula for your library. Do your research first—how long can such an animal go without care in case of an emergency? Might there be any smells associated with this pet? Health hazards such as allergies? What do they eat?

Once you're sure that you can safely care for a library pal at your desk (best to keep Kermit or Nemo where you can keep an eye on them), you're good to go with a variety of passive programs.

- Name Our Fish (or hamster or frog or turtle).
- Observation Log: Very important work—what time of day did you make your observation, and exactly what was Khaleesi the Cuttlefish doing? We love the idea of collecting observation data and eventually turning it into a Day in the Life chart.
- Make up an adventure for Mr. Whiskers.
- Draw a picture of Leo the Library Lizard.
- Fact challenge: Tell a library staff member one interesting fact about guinea pigs to win feeding or petting privileges.
- Turtle Trivia: Answer questions about turtles in general or Percy Turtle in specific.
- True or False: Facts and misconceptions about tarantulas.

A living, breathing library pet is a long shot for many venues—weekends, holidays, and weather closures can spell catastrophe for your little friend, and there must be room for food, bedding, and veterinary care in your budget. Firm rules about handling the critter and tapping on its cage must be established and enforced. Having a pet, either in the library or in your home, is a serious commitment. Only take it on if you are aware of and prepared for the responsibilities involved.

Adopt a . . .

If you've considered the factors and just can't make a real pet work in your library, how about adopting a tree outside the library? The same passive programming can be created—a name contest, trivia, true or false, observations—including making up silly adventures for Lady Birch or Ms. Greenleaf.

Alternatively, a staff member may own a pet that can visit the library on a regular basis, and you can plan passive programs to supplement. We know of one library that has regular Bunny Saturdays. Awww!

Reading readiness circuit for caregivers and kids

Think of this as circuit training for tiny minds—a series of activities that caregivers can do with babies and toddlers that are not only fun but also good for baby's brain.

Parents and caregivers are often a bit at sea when it comes to knowing what kinds of play contribute to reading readiness. At the very least, many could use some validation that the ways that they play with their baby are valuable—most engage in early literacy reading readiness activities without even thinking about it. "What color is baby's shirt?" It's nice to post information about what they're doing right.

Print instructions for reading readiness activities such as color matching, shape sorting, wooden puzzles, and the like. Post these in sign holders in the baby area. Number each sign to give caregivers a way to track their progress—not that this is particularly important, but it can be a helpful motivator. Add information about what each activity is doing to foster prereading skills in the child, and finish with a quick cheery statement about reading with their child every day.

An Early Learning Station suggests a reading readiness activity for caregivers.

You could buy a set of signs like these from an educational supply house, but homemade ones with your library's logo and storytime schedule will have more of an impact. Since these activities are more or less evergreen, you might request professionally made signs from your system's graphics department.

Reading readiness activities

- How high can you stack the blocks?
- Can you make a pattern with the linking toys?
- Roll the giant die. Can you clap that many times?

INSTANT REPLAY:

A teen girl reads aloud the poem
Harlem by Langston Hughes
for the Poetry Month challenge.

Her: "I don't get it. What's it about?"

Me: [defines "deferred," then walks her through the poem, line by line]

Her: "Oh! I get it now! He's saying don't put off your dreams or they'll dry up and explode! That's really good advice. Why didn't he just say that?"

9

The Whole Nine Yards: A Year of Inspiration

Oh, how we librarians love our monthly themes! There are limitless passive programs you can create to tie in with your other seasonal displays and decorations.

But while active programs are generally designed for wide appeal—cookie decorating in December, mask making in October—passive programming lets you celebrate holidays that are not as well known in your community, or holidays observed by just a few families at your library. Highlighting holidays celebrated by people all over the world fosters knowledge, awareness, and inclusivity and can engage members of your community who may not expect to see themselves at the library.

Be respectful and solicit input from local leaders and cultural groups. When it comes to the traditions of cultures that are not our own, be aware that we often don't know what we don't know.

Kooky calendar observances such as National Popcorn Day (January 19) and Make Up Your Own Holiday Day (March 26) also help feed your passive programming habit.

World holidays

Holidays celebrated by people around the world are a great excuse to prompt a little cultural awareness education. They add color and excitement to otherwise drab months. We've added Diwali, the Chinese Moon Festival, Dia de los Muertos, and a dozen others to our calendar below, and shared lists of relevant books. Refer to the following easy ways to leverage your library materials so that you can roll out passive programming for almost any holiday anywhere in the world at the drop of a *kepi*.

Fact challenge

Pair a display of nonfiction books on the country, fiction set in that country or written by authors whose heritage reflects it, as well as folk tales and any books you have in that country's language with a prompt: Share a fact you learned about this place with your family or friends. Customers who share their new fact with library staff earn a little prize.

Find a fact egg hunt

Collect, type up, and print country facts on slips of paper. Stuff the slips in plastic eggs and hide them around the library. Anyone who brings a fact to a library staff member and reads it wins a prize. Display the found eggs in a basket at the desk along with a sign announcing your egg hunt or ask your seekers to re-hide the eggs they've found. Be ready with lots of facts—an egg hunter motivated by the promise of stickers or candy can find a lot of eggs fairly quickly.

Say Hi

Post a common greeting along with its translation and pronunciation. Anyone who says hi to a library staff member in that language gets a prize!

Write your name

Display a non-Latin alphabet along with transliterated English characters and a whiteboard or chalkboard challenge: Write your name in Greek (or Amharic or Hebrew or Malayalam)! See the appendix for online resources that make this program easy to set up.

Heritage or History Months

These tried and true ideas can be adapted for any celebration of heritage and history. They are easily resupplied and durable enough to last a whole month. Our examples refer to Black History Month, but you'll want to try these during Women's History Month, Hispanic Heritage Month, Asian Pacific American Heritage Month, Jewish Heritage Month, and more.

ID challenge

Great for a bulletin board or wall—post photos of prominent Black Americans and ask customers identify their names and accomplishments. Number the photos and make it a match game, with answer sheets to be turned in for a prize or as an Enter to Win entry. No bulletin board? Make a worksheet.

Find the famous folks

Post pictures and thumbnail bios of notable Black people throughout your library. Print the same pictures at a smaller size on scavenger hunt sheets and challenge customers not only to find the matching pictures but to write down something interesting about each individual. This perennial favorite comes from librarian Kelly Burden at Enoch Pratt Free Library's Southeast Anchor Library.

My inspiration

We love this idea for its extendibility. Use your whiteboard or bulletin board as a space for customers to contribute names of people who inspire them. Then use that list to create a book display, a garland of photos, or to guide other programming centered on the group that is being celebrated.

Book or library appreciation days

Reading is global

List languages and provide the translation for "I am a reader" in each. If you do this on an interactive board, be sure to leave lots of space for customers to contribute additional translations!

This has been a big hit every time we've put it up. Customers have added translations in Hindi, Bengali, Urdu, Yoruba, Amharic, Turkish, and more!

TABLE 9.1

Observance	Slogan
National Readaloud Day	I am a reader
National Library Week	I love my library
Banned Books Week	I read banned books
Dia de los Niños	Read

January

New Year's Day

In this coming year I want to . . .

New Year's resolutions are a no-brainer writing prompt, but we like wording the question in a way that leaves room for dreams and aspirations without the pressure of resolve. Post this question on your board or drawing table or try one of the following.

Big Jar

Provide slips for customers to make their little promises to themselves and drop in the jar. You can leave the jar open so that they can sample the good intentions of others, too!

Garland or mobile

A chain or tree of resolutions is a lovely idea. Provide colored paper strips and fancy pens to make the chain, or stars to hang from a tree.

Lunar New Year

Fact Challenge, Say Hi, and Write Your Name all work well for Lunar New Year, which is celebrated in China, Japan, Vietnam (where it's called Tết), and Korea (Seollal). There are a wide variety of new year's traditions to draw from.

The demographics of your library population may inspire tailor-made passive programs with lots of local appeal. Try a Write Your Name challenge or one of these animal programs based on the Chinese zodiac.

Chinese Zodiac activities

Post a chart of the Chinese zodiac. Find the year you were born, then write or draw your zodiac animal. Read about the characteristics of that zodiac sign. How are you like or unlike that animal? This is a great activity that prompts questions about Chinese culture and gives kids and adults a little practice reading a chart.

WHITEBOARD, CHALKBOARD, OR BULLETIN BOARD

Find a circular Chinese zodiac chart and post it on your board. Use skinny washi tape to extend the lines between the zodiac signs to the edges of the board. Provide markers so that customers can add their names in the spaces around the zodiac that correspond to their birth year.

MAKE A WISH FOR NEW YEAR

This makes a great whiteboard prompt or lovely additions to a garland or mobile.

BIG JAR

Fill your jar with slips printed with the animals of the zodiac. Challenge customers to pick a slip and then find a book or other type of materials featuring that animal in the library.

PASSPORT PROGRAM

Read your way through the Chinese zodiac. Start this one on January 1 and see if your customers can read about each of the twelve zodiac animals by the time Chinese New Year rolls around. This is a great way to extend the holiday season, and to make a point about the difference between Lunar New Year and New Year on the Western calendar.

ACTIVITY SHEET

Chinese zodiac challenge: a page with each of the Chinese zodiac animals and challenge customers to read or watch something about each of those animals. Or just feature the animal that represents the current year and task users to find five facts about that animal.

Zodiac Challenge booklist

TABLE 9.2

Chinese zodiac symbol	Sample titles
Rat	*Oh, Rats!* by Albert Marrin
	Cyril and Pat by Emily Gravett
	Fergus and Zeke by Kate Messner
Ox (or cow)	*14 Cows for America* by Carmen Agra Deedy
	The Big Fat Cow That Went Kapow by Andy Griffiths
	Ferdinand by Munro Leaf
	Bully by Laura Vaccaro Seeger
Tiger	*When You Trap a Tiger* by Tae Keller
	Don't Wake Up the Tiger by Britta Teckentrup
	Tiger vs. Nightmare by Emily Tetri
	Camp Tiger by Susan Choi
Rabbit	*Hey Rabbit!* By Sergio Ruzzier
	Wolfie Bunny by Ame Dyckman
	Mr. and Mrs. Bunny by Polly Horvath
Dragon	*Raising Dragons* by Jerdine Nolen
	Snoring Beauty by Bruce Hale
	Dragons in a Bag by Zetta Elliott
	Dragon Hoops by Gene Luen Yang
	The Dragon Slayer: Folktales from Latin America by Jaime Hernandez
	Game of Thrones (series) by George R. R. Martin

(continued)

TABLE 9.2 (*Continued*)

Chinese zodiac symbol	Sample titles
Snake	*Verdi* by Janell Cannon
	Hide and Snake by Keith Baker
	Snakes on a Train by Kathryn Dennis
	The White Snake by Ben Nadler
Horse	*The Girl Who Loved Wild Horses* by Paul Goble
	Bunny the Brave War Horse by Elizabeth MacLeod
	Riding Freedom by Pam Munoz Ryan
	War Horse by Michael Morpurgo
Monkey	*Hug* by Jez Alborough
	Never Smile at a Monkey by Steve Jenkins
	Summer of the Monkeys by Wilson Rawls
Goat (or sheep)	*Grumpy Goat* by Brett Helquist
	Sheep in a Jeep by Nancy Shaw
Rooster	*Minerva Louise* by Janet Morgan Stoeke
	Chicken in the Kitchen by Nnedi Okorafor
	I Got a Chicken for My Birthday by Laura Gehl
	The Chicken Squad books by Doreen Cronin
	Unusual Chickens for the Exceptional Poultry Farmer by Kelly Jones
Dog	*Skippyjon Jones* by Judy Schachner
	How to Steal a Dog by Barbara O'Connor
	Dog Man by Dav Pilkey
	Call of the Wild by Jack London
Pig	*Pigaroons* by Arthur Geisert
	Olivia by Ian Falconer
	Charlotte's Web by E.B. White
	Mercy Watson (series) by Kate DiCamillo
	What This Story Needs Is a Pig in a Wig by Emma J. Virjan
	Animal Farm by George Orwell

Fact Challenge booklist for Lunar New Year. Look for the All About . . . series (Tuttle), *National Geographic*'s Countries of the World books and Lonely Planet Kids titles, as well as these great books about lunar new year:

> *Chinese New Year: A Celebration for Everyone* by Jen Sookfong Lee
> *The Great Race: The Story of the Chinese Zodiac* by Christopher Corr

Golden Blooms: Celebrating Tet-Vietnamese Lunar New Year by Y. T. Tran

This Next New Year by Janet S. Wong

Nian: The Chinese New Year Dragon by Virginia Loh-Hagan

Crouching Tiger by Ying Chang Compestine

Diary of a Tokyo Teen: A Japanese-American Girl Travels to the Land of Trendy Fashion, High-Tech Toilets and Maid Cafes by Christine Mari Inzer

Martin Luther King Jr. Day

Writing prompt

Dear Dr. King: What would you ask or say to Dr. Martin Luther King, Jr. if you had the chance? Pair this with Nic Stone's *Dear Martin*.

I have a dream

Provide cloud shapes on which customers can inscribe their dreams. If you have the space, put out glitter glue, cotton balls, and sticker stars to decorate the clouds—everyone knows dreams come true if you douse them with glitter! Then hang these dreams on your mobile, garland, bulletin board, or other vertical space.

Biographies and more

Memphis, Martin, and the Mountaintop: The Sanitation Strike of 1968 by Alice Faye Duncan

Dear Martin by Nic Stone

Martin Rising: Requiem For a King by Andrea Davis Pinkney

When Marian Sang by Pam Munoz Ryan

A Place to Land: Martin Luther King Jr. and the Speech That Inspired a Nation by Barry Wittenstein

Basant

Basant, or Festival of Kites, is observed by Hindus and Sikhs in late January to early February. It celebrates the first day of spring and the goddess Saraswati. Kites, the color yellow, and expressions of romantic love are all associated with Basant. Take a look at *King for a Day* by Rukhsana Khan to learn more about Basant.

On the craft table

Stock your craft table with yellow paper and instructions on how to make a variety of paper flowers, or put out a kite craft.

Writing prompt

If I were a kite, I'd fly to. . . .

February

Black History Month

Keep your list of extraordinary Black Americans up to date. Be sure to include scientists, inventors, and political figures as well as athletes and entertainers. This might seem to go without saying, but kids still come into the library brandishing lists from their teachers that include Wilt Chamberlain but not Barack Obama.

Your main passive program might be ID Challenge, Find the Famous Folks, My Inspiration (details above), or a Black History trivia contest, but here are a few ideas specific to Black History Month.

A few favorite books for Black History Month

> *We Are Not Yet Equal: Understanding Our Racial Divide* by Carol Anderson and Tonya Bolden
> *Trombone Shorty* by Troy Andrews
> *The Youngest Marcher: The Story of Audrey Faye Hendricks, a Young Civil Rights Activist* by Cynthia Levinson
> *Dave the Potter: Artist, Poet, Slave* by Laban Carrick Hill
> *The Case for Loving: The Fight for Interracial Marriage* by Selina Alko and Sean Qualls
> *Ruth and the Green Book* by Calvin Alexander Ramsey
> *Bad News for Outlaws: The Remarkable Life of Bass Reeves, Deputy U.S. Marshal* by Vaunda Micheaux Nelson
> *Jazz Day: The Making of a Famous Photograph* by Roxane Orgill
> *Radiant Child: The Story of Young Artist Jean-Michel Basquiat* by Javaka Steptoe
> *Schomburg: The Man Who Built a Library* by Carole Boston Weatherford

Unity wreath

Put out construction paper in "multicultural" hues and invite library visitors to trace their hand on the color that they identify most strongly with. Or provide precut hands in a variety of colors for kids too young to use scissors. Decorate with markers and provide a basket or box for finished hands. Because the hand shapes resemble leaves, they look great dangling from a tree branch display or glued to a wreath form or paper plates to make large or small wreaths.

At Paula's library, this activity taught us a sad lesson on colorism and how early it is internalized. Some three- and four-year-old Latina girls rejected the colors that most resembled their own skin, instead picking paper in the lightest shade available, describing it as "the prettiest." You can bet that our next bilingual storytime featured some of the following books.

Making hands for the Unity Wreath at Paula's library.

> *I Am Perfectly Designed* by Karamo Brown, Jason "Rachel" Brown, Anoosha Syed
> *Hair Love* by Matthew A. Cherry
> *Parker Looks Up: An Extraordinary Moment* by Parker Curry, Jessica Curry, Brittany Jackson
> *Honeysmoke: A Story of Finding Your Color* by Monique Fields, Yesenia Moises
> *The Skin I'm In* by Sharon G. Flake
> *Not Quite Snow White* by Ashley Franklin, Ebony Glenn
> *Skin Again* by bell hooks and Chris Raschka
> *Black Is a Rainbow Color* by Angela Joy
> *Sulwe* by Lupita Nyong'o
> *Genesis Begins Again* by Alicia D. Williams
> *Pecan Pie Baby* by Jaqueline Woodson

Harry Potter Book Night

Celebrated in the first week of February, this is often the annual holiday generates the most excitement among library staff.

Draw your patronus

Print a chart (easily found on the Internet) of patronuses and their personalities and ask readers to imagine what their own patronus would be and draw it. This works just as well on a whiteboard as on an activity sheet.

What's your Hogwarts House?

Put up a big square divided into four parts, each area labeled with the name of a Hogwarts residence hall: Hufflepuff, Gryffindor, Slytherin, and Ravenclaw. Invite customers to self-identify by adding a magnet, a tick mark, their name, or a sticker to the appropriate area.

You can print or provide a link to an online quiz that they can do on their phone in order to reveal their house affiliation, but most Harry Potter fans already know which house they identify with.

Photobooth 9¾

Line a secluded nook with brick-patterned contact paper or make a back-drop using roll paper and a rectangular sponge dipped in paint to make brick shapes. Load a book cart with suitcases (bonus if you can find a birdcage that you can stuff an owl puppet into!). Use an inexpensive clip-on light to make the spot feel special and the photos well-lit.

Be sure your library's logo and hashtag are graffitied on the "brick" wall so that when customers post their selfie to Instagram everyone can see that they were hanging out with the cool kids at the library.

Valentine's Day

Romance novel cover captions

Romance novel covers are often unquestionably silly. Post color copies of a few covers and ask customers to submit hilarious captions. Or, use image editing software to remove the titles and solicit original title ideas.

You'll never look at a Western romance the same way again once some kid has changed the title from "Cowboy Hearts" to "Cowboy Farts." (True story. She also drew a speech balloon for the horse and wrote "I farted too." The rewards of this job are many.)

Conversation candy hearts

Use construction paper hearts, or draw hearts on your board or drawing table, and invite customers to write in their original sentiment. In the children's department, be prepared for more fart jokes.

What do you call your schmoopy pie?

A great writing prompt for a whiteboard or chalkboard: Pet, best friend, family member, or loved one—what silly name do you call your beloved? This also makes a lovely seasonal garland or mobile—provide paper hearts or, even better, repurpose used Valentines (just cut along the fold and discard the back).

Spring

Kindness garden

Cut out a variety of flower shapes from construction paper. Participants write a kind or encouraging thought on their flower and post it on a bulletin board, mobile, garland, or other space in your library.

Seed match challenge

Choose five or more seeds in a variety of shapes and sizes, and then find pictures of the plants that they will grow into.

The easiest way to do this is to glue the seeds to a sheet of paper, circle them with a marker (some seeds are extremely small!), and number them. You can then color

Too cool for Valentine's Day in the teen department.

copy this sheet or post it on your board along with pictures of the plants.

Level up by making this a three-way match challenge—match the seed to the photo to the name of the plant!

Food or foe?

Some plants are edible and others are poison. Google "common edible plants of (your region)" and "common poisonous plants of (same region)." Print photos of both types labeled with their scientific and common names and post them to your board. Challenge customers to identify which is which.

Growing things booklist

A Seed is Sleepy by Dianna Hutts Aston
Planting a rainbow by Lois Ehlert

How Groundhog's Garden Grew by Lynne Cherry
Underground by Denise Fleming
In the Garden by Emma Giuliani
Up in the garden and down in the dirt by Kate Messner
Easy Peasy: Gardening for Kids by Kirsten Bradley
Spring After Spring: How Rachel Carson Inspired the Environmental Movement
    by Stephanie Roth Sisson
City Green by DyAnne DiSalvo-Ryan

March

Women's History Month

If you're like us, programming centered on women's history just seems to design itself. We start early to fit it all in, adding a little extra oomph on March 8, International Women's Day. Put up an ID Challenge, Find the Famous Folks scavenger hunt, or a My Inspiration prompt. See the beginning of this chapter for detailed instructions on these passive programs.

Writing prompts

WOMEN MAKE THE BEST . . .

Fried chicken? Senators? Crafts? Book recommendations? How about all the above?

NAME THREE FAMOUS (OR NOT-FAMOUS) WOMEN YOU'D LIKE TO HAVE DINNER WITH

We know you can put together a display of biographies of women from all walks of life, but here are a few recent favorites that will inspire ideas of spirited dinner conversation.

What Do You Do with a Voice Like That?: The Story of Extraordinary Congress-woman Barbara Jordan by Chris Barton
Game Changers: The Story of Venus and Serena Williams by Lesa Cline-Ransome
The Book of Gutsy Women: Favorite Stories of Courage and Resilience by Hillary Rodham Clinton and Chelsea Clinton
She Came to Slay: The Life and Times of Harriet Tubman by Erica Armstrong Dunbar
Little Leaders by Vashti Harrison
Shaking Things Up: 14 Young Women Who Changed the World by Susan Hood
Amazons, Abolitionists, and Activists: A Graphic History of Women's Fight for Their Rights by Mikki Kendall

Miss Mary Reporting: The True Story of Sportswriter Mary Garber by Sue Macy

The Lady from the Black Lagoon: Hollywood Monsters and the Lost Legacy of Milicent Patrick by Mallory O'Meara

Toil & Trouble: 15 Tales of Women & Witchcraft by Tess Sharpe

Grace Hopper: Queen of Computer Code by Laurie Wallmark

The World Is Not a Rectangle: A Portrait of Architect Zaha Hadid by Jeannette Winter

My favorite season is awards season

Take advantage of the media attention surrounding the Golden Globes, Emmys, Tonys, and the Oscars by building passive programming around books that have been made into movies, Broadway shows, and TV. Chances are, the books that this year's award contenders are based on will all be checked out, but you can post match games on your board or make activity sheets.

Of course you can always hold a "Mock Oscar" and provide a list of nominees in various categories and see how your customers' choices compare with the Academy's, but you're in a library—why not tie it to books?

Working title

Many books get a new title when they are adapted. Sometimes these are obvious and sometimes not, but this makes a fun match game.

Examples:

Field of Dreams—Shoeless Joe by W. P. Kinsella

Willy Wonka and the Chocolate Factory—Charlie and the Chocolate Factory by Roald Dahl

Goodfellas—Wiseguy by Nicholas Pileggi

Apocalypse Now—Heart of Darkness by Joseph Conrad

Stand By Me—"The Body" by Stephen King

There Will be Blood—Oil! By Upton Sinclair

Slumdog Millionaire—Q&A by Vikas Swarup

Blade Runner—"Do Androids Dream of Electric Sheep?" by Philip K. Dick

Cruel Intentions—Les Liaisons Dangereuses by Choderlos de Laclos

Adaptation—The Orchid Thief by Susan Orleans

Anne with an E—Anne of Green Gables by L.M. Montgomery

Match the cover to the poster

Use image editing software (or construction paper) to obscure the title on images of book covers. Challenge players to match the book to the movie poster. Try to include a mixture of new, classic, popular, and lesser-known examples—we've picked a few good ones below. OBVIOUSLY, you don't want to use cover art from the movie tie-in edition of the book for this activity, because what would be the point?

What to Expect When You're Expecting
The Dark Knight
Like Water for Chocolate
Hidden Figures
Fast Times at Ridgemont High
Forrest Gump
I Am Legend
World War Z
The Jungle Book
The Princess Bride
Holes
Rosemary's Baby
The Godfather

That's not how I pictured them

Find pictures of actors in character as the roles they played in movies or shows based on books and challenge library visitors to match the image to the character name. Extra points for multiple depictions (how many Jo Marshes and Dr. Watsons can you find?)!

Viola Davis as Rose Maxson (*Fences* by August Wilson)
Peter Dinklage as Tyrion Lannister (the Game of Thrones novels by George R.R. Martin)
Ralph Fiennes as Voldemort (the Harry Potter novels by J. K. Rowling)
Kathryn Heigl as Stephanie Plum (the Stephanie Plum novels by Janet Evanovich)
Mindy Kaling as Mrs. Who (A *Wrinkle in Time* by Madeleine L'Engle
Jack Nicholson as Jack Torrance (*The Shining* by Stephen King)
Stephen Strait as Jim Holden (the Expanse novels by James S. A. Corey)
Meryl Streep as Julia Child (*Julie and Julia* by Julie Powell)
Denzel Washington as Easy Rawlins (the Easy Rawlins novels by Walter Mosley)
Amandla Stenberg as Starr (*The Hate U Give* by Angie Thomas)

Argungu Fishing Festival (Nigeria)

Obscure? Not to your West African customers. During this four-day festival, fishermen gather on the banks of the Sokoto River, competing to catch the biggest fish using only handmade nets. Irresistible!

Gone fishing—on a wall, window, or garland

Make a river on a wall or bulletin board out of roll paper. Print a short description of the festival. Provide fish shapes for customers to decorate and add to your river. No wall? Use a window, with blue tissue paper for the river and tulle or gauze for nets. No window? Make a garland to hang your fish on—be sure to add information cards to various spots on the garland.

Contest: Write a "fish story"

One term for a tall tale is a fish story—as in "I once caught a fish THIS BIG. . . ." There are tips for stretching the imagination with tall tale activities in chapter 7, and here are some prompts you can use specifically for Argungu:

> As I was walking along the river, I looked down and saw. . . .
> I had a magic fishing net that always caught. . . .
> I once caught a fish so big that. . . .

Stories from West Africa booklist

Why Mosquitoes Buzz in People's Ears: A West African Tale by Verna Aardema
Baby Goes to Market by Atinuke
A Is for Africa by Ifeoma Onyefulu
Nana Akua Goes to School by Tricia Elam Walker
The Water Princess by Susan Verde
Ikenga by Nnedi Okorafor
Tristan Strong Punches a Hole in the Sky by Kwame Mbalia
Chicken in the Kitchen by Nnedi Okorafor
My Name is Konisola by Alisa Siegel

Mardi Gras/Carnival

The colors and music of spring festivals perk up what can be a drab month. All three of these holidays involve masks and costumes—why should October get all the dress-up fun? Stock your craft table with blank masks, markers, craft feathers, and adhesive gems.

Carnival and Mardi Gras bookspirations

Camila Quiere Escribir by Matilde García-Arroyo and Hilda E. Quintana
Petite Rouge by Mike Artell
Rafi and Rosi Carnival! by Lulu Delacre
Gator Gumbo by Candace Fleming
Drummer Boy of John John by Mark Greenwood
Malaika's Costume by Nadia L. Hohn
Jump Up Time by Lynn Joseph
Dancing at Carnival by Christine Platt

Purim

Books for Purim:

On Purim by Cathy Goldberg Fishman
The Story of Queen Esther by Jenny Koralek
The Purim Superhero by Elisabeth Kushner
Sammy Spider's First Purim by Sylvia A. Rouss
Barnyard Purim by Kelly Terwilliger

Happy Holi

Holi is celebrated with a festival of color. Hindus and Sikhs celebrate Holi.

Writing/drawing prompt

Buy a new set of bright colored whiteboard markers or chalk and use your whiteboard to ask "What's your favorite color?" Level up by asking what that color means to them: "Yellow is a bumblebee buzzing in the sunshine."

Craft table

Supply your craft table with colored paper and ornament stencils. Hang finished paper ornaments on your mobile or garland.

Colorful booklist:

Chromatopia: An Illustrated History of Color by David Cole
The Black Book of Colors by Menena Cottin

The Many Colors of Harpreet Singh by Supriya Kelkar
Andy Warhol: What Colors Do You See? By Mudpuppy
Pantone: Colors
Mix it Up by Herve Tullet
Festival of Colors by Surishtha Sehgal
Holi Colors by Rina Singh

Dr. Seuss Day

What kind of Dr. Seuss creature are you?

Create two correlation charts—month you were born/Seussian adjectives and color of your socks/Seuss creatures. You might be a Tizzle-topped Kwuggerbug!

TABLE 9.3

Month you were born		Color of your socks	
January	Tizzle-topped	Red	Thwerll
February	Tackleberry	Orange	Lorax
March	Bean-shooter	Yellow	Mazurka
April	Carnivorous	Green	Skritz
May	Green-headed	Blue	Jicker
June	Horn-tooter	Purple	Slippard
July	High-jumping	Brown	Grickle
August	Squirmulous	Black	Kwuggerbug
September	Gicky	White	Poozer
October	Grinchy	Multi	Joat
November	Key-slapping		
December	Perilous		

Naturally, you'll want to post a display of Dr. Seuss books nearby.

April

April Fools' Day

Find a joke

Our favorite egg hunt produces a lot of hilarity and groans. Stuff your plastic eggs with family-friendly jokes and hide them all over your library. While jokes are undeniably fun and silly and less mean-spirited than pranks, they also teach kids about wordplay, especially homonyms and other puns. Level up by including jokes in languages other than English.

Q: Que hace un pece?
A: Nada!

National Poetry Month

Magnetic poetry

Buy a kit or make your own using magnetic tape. Use a magnetic board (some whiteboards are magnetic), the sides of book carts, or metal panels available at craft stores for workspaces. This is a great one for sharing—add your library's hashtag when you take the picture and post completed poems to a bulletin board or on social media.

Examples of blackout poetry are displayed along with raw materials and customer contributions.

Blackout poetry

We love eking one last use out of much-loved withdrawn books. Using them to make blackout poetry is a great one. Blackout poems are "written" by coloring over all the words on the page with a black marker—except for the few that make up your poem.

Tear out some pages and put them in a basket. Post a sample of the format and a can of black markers. Give

customers vertical space, a mobile or a garland so that they can display their completed poems.

Poetry trivia

Print selected lines from classic and contemporary poems onto strips of paper and stuff them into your Big Jar. Customers draw a random slip and are challenged to look up the name of the poem and the poet. For an extra prize, they can read the poem aloud to you. This is a favorite passive program in Andria's Teen Lounge because young people reading poetry to us always brightens our day. Oh, and it fosters literacy and a love of language in the teens, too!

Passport to poetry

Here's a passport program for Poetry Month. Every time someone presents you with a poem (bonus for reading it aloud!), you punch their card.

Level this up by challenging library users to find and read a poem that fits each of the following poetic forms:

Haiku
Cinquain
Concrete poetry
Free verse
Limerick
Ode
Sestina
Sijo
Sonnet
Tanka

Ransom note poetry

Here's a two-parter: Put out a bin of old magazines and a couple pairs of scissors, along with a sign asking customers to find and cut out fun words from headlines and ads. Once you have accumulated a box full of words, switch out the scissors for glue sticks and blank paper and encourage visitors to compose their own poetry—or, as one of Andria's teen customers did—their own actual ransom notes.

Book spine poetry

> *"Where is the Green Sheep?"*
> *"Maybe a Bear Ate It"*
> —*Paula's favorite book spine poem*

If you only have a shelf or a small display to devote to Poetry Month passive programs, make the most of it with book spine poetry! The rules are easy: compose a poem in which every line is the title of a book. Stack the books so that the poem reads from the top down. Use any combination of books in the library and leave your stack on the shelf or table.

Naturally, this activity can mess with shelving and searching, so sweep this area a few times a day to collect the books for reshelving—after you photograph each creation. Post these images to inspire more participation. Add your library hashtag and share on social media!

May

Jewish American Heritage Month

Jewish community associations or education centers are great library partners. They can often provide informed library programs or suggest ideas.

Micrography craft

Micrography is the art of using calligraphy skills to create images or symbols out of letters and words. Provide intricate stencils and examples and see what your library users come up with!

Along with the winners of the Sydney Taylor Book Award and the National Jewish Book Awards, here are a few books to highlight. Jewish history is not just the Holocaust—make sure your offerings highlight triumphs as well as tragedy.

> *A Place at the Table* by Saadia Faruqi and Laura Shovan
> *The Mountain Jews and the Mirror* by Ruchama Feuerman
> *The Book Rescuer: How a Mensch from Massachusetts Saved Yiddish Literature for Generations to Come* by Sue Macy
> *Gittel's Journey: An Ellis Island Story* by Lesléa Newman
> *All Three Stooges* by Erica S. Perl
> *Regina Persisted: An Untold Story* by Sandy Eisenberg Sasso
> *Raisel's Riddle* by Erica Silverman
> *The Length of a String* by Elissa Brent Weissman

And There Was Evening, and There Was Morning by Ellen Kahan Zager and
　　Harriet Helfand
A Moon for Moe and Mo by Jane Breskin Zalben

International Workers Day

International Workers Day is celebrated on May 1. It's a great moment to roll
out a "What Do You Want to Be When You Grow Up" prompt—or, for adults,
"What DID You Want to be When You Grew Up?"

Pop this question on a whiteboard or chalkboard, or provide paper shapes
that customers can label with their profession of choice and add to a garland
or mobile. (As for your authors, Andria wanted to be a pediatrician, and Paula
assumed she'd grow up to be president. There's still time!)

Golden Week (Japan)

The Golden Week is a collection of four national holidays within seven days:
Showa Day (Showa no hi), the birthday of former Emperor Showa; Consti-
tution Day (Kenpo kinenbi); Greenery Day (Midori no hi), dedicated to the
environment and nature; and Children's Day (Kodomo no hi).

It's one of Japan's three busiest holiday seasons (along with New Year
and the Obon week). Celebrate all things Japanese during this week in
early May.

Writing prompts

If I were emperor, I would. . . .
On Children's Day, children should get to. . . .
What's one thing we can do to protect the environment?

How to bow

Bowing in Japan varies according to the situation. Play this cute instructional
video (https://youtu.be/ytmdQC6OxPU) on your monitor and reward anyone
who bows to a library staff member with a prize or special bookmark. Don't
forget to bow in response!

Free Comic Book Day/May the Fourth Be With You

The pop culture section in chapter 7 has many ideas that can be adapted for
these celebrations, and also see Star Wars Reads Day under the October head-
ing of this chapter.

Flying, teleportation, or immortality? So many powers, so little room on this popular whiteboard prompt.

Height chart

Height charts, described in chapter 7, are fun any time but are a natural fit with anything sci-fi or comics related. Even smallish children will discover that they're taller than Rocket Raccoon (3'1") or Yoda (2'2").

Rewrite the comics

Photocopy pages from graphic novels and comic books and white out the text and conversation bubbles. Invite customers to imagine new conversations and original ways to interpret the images for an activity that fosters both visual and verbal literacy.

Button making

Bring out that button maker if you have one, and let customers make buttons from the pages of discarded comic books and Star Wars graphic novels.

Cinco de Mayo

Invite customers to make a stack of books in the colors of the Mexican flag. Set the stacks out adjacent to a display of books by or about Mexicans or Mexican Americans, or photograph them and reshelve. Extra points for using books with appropriate thematic content!

Lista de libros sobre temas mexicanas:

Frida Kahlo and her animalitos by Monica Brown
Tamalitos and other books by Jorge Argueta
Caramelos by Sandra Cisneros
The Diary of Frida Kahlo: An Intimate Self-Portrait
Malinche by Laura Esquivel
Había una vez mexicanas que hicieron historia by Pedro J. Fernández

¡Vamos! Let's Go to the Market by Raúl the Third
Danza!: Amalia Hernández and El Ballet Folklórico de México by Duncan Tonatiuh
Dear Primo by Duncan Tonatiuh

African Liberation Day

This pan-African holiday is celebrated on May 25.

Timeline challenge

Pick 10 or 12 African countries and list them out of order alongside the year that they became independent and/or the country that formerly ruled them.

Match games

FLAG TO COUNTRY OR CAPITAL CITY TO COUNTRY

There are 54 countries in Africa—we suggest dividing them into groups and assigning each group a level. Big prizes for anyone who can finish all the levels!

CAPITAL CITY NAMES, THEIR MEANING, AND THEIR LANGUAGE OF ORIGIN

TABLE 9.4

City name	Meaning or derivation of name
1. Accra (Ghana)	A. From an Akan word meaning "ants"
2. Antananarivo (Madagascar)	B. "City of the thousand" in Malagasy
3. Bamako (Mali)	C. From a Bambara word meaning "river of crocodiles"
4. Cape Town (South Africa)	D. British English
5. Dar es Salaam (Tanzania)	E. "Home of peace" in Arabic
6. Harare (Zimbabwe)	F. Named after a chief whose name meant "he who does not sleep" in Shona
7. Kampala (Uganda)	G. From a Luganda translation of the British name, "Hills of the Impala"
8. Mogadishu (Somalia)	H. Said to derive from a Persian phrase meaning "seat of the Shah"
9. Ouagadougou (Burkina Faso)	I. French transliteration of a Mossi word meaning "Come honor me" (Wogdo)
10. Porto-Novo (Benin)	J. "New port" in Portuguese
11. Praia (Cape Verde)	K. "Beach" in Portuguese
12. Windhoek (Namibia)	L. "Wind corner" in Afrikaans

Find these stories and many more on the blog afrolegends.com.

LANDMARK TO COUNTRY

TABLE 9.5

Landmark	Location
1. Mount Kilimanjaro	A. Tanzania
2. Djemaa el Fna	B. Morocco
3. Sossusvlei Dunes	C. Namibia
4. Table Mountain	D. South Africa
5. Victoria Falls	E. Zambia/Zimbabwe
6. Pyramids	F. Egypt
7. Nyiragongo Volcano	G. Democratic Republic of Congo
8. Fish River Canyon	H. Namibia
9. Lake Retba	I. Senegal
10. Lalibela	J. Ethiopia
11. Zuma Rock	K. Nigeria

African Liberation Day bookspirations:

Ashley Bryan's African Tales, Uh-Huh
Mama Africa!: How Miriam Makeba Spread Hope with Her Song by Kathryn Erskine
Jambo Means Hello: Swahili Alphabet Book by Muriel L. Feelings
Africa Is Not a Country by Margy Burns Knight
Mama Miti: Wangari Maathai and the Trees of Kenya by Donna Jo Napoli
Born a Crime by Trevor Noah
Nya's Long Walk: A Step at a Time by Linda Sue Park
One Plastic Bag: Isatou Ceesay and the Recycling Women of the Gambia by Miranda Paul
Emmanuel's Dream: The True Story of Emmanuel Ofosu Yeboah by Laurie Ann Thompson
The Water Princess by Susan Verde, Georgie Badiel, and Peter H. Reynolds

Eid

Eid al-Fitr falls in late May or early June. It's an important holiday celebrated by Muslims around the world, marking the end of the holy month of Ramadan.

Pay attention to the demographics of your community—Islam is very diverse, not to mention geographically widespread. Customs vary from place to place. Do you have a significant Somali or Nigerian population in your area? Is there a large Moroccan, Indonesian, or Pakistani community?

Look up how holidays are celebrated in the various countries the Muslims who visit your library may hail from. For example, South Asian Muslims often apply mehndi (henna) to hands and feet during Eid—you'll find instructions for a mehndi craft under Diwali (October). Better yet, partner with a local Muslim community group and ask *them* what they'd like to see in the library during major holidays.

The following activities are general enough, however, to work no matter what.

"What do you eat to celebrate a special occasion?"

Many Muslims fast during the month of Ramadan, and celebrate Eid al-Fitr, the end of the holy month, with a big feast. We like this inclusive prompt for the way it draws everyone in. Lots of people celebrate special occasions and holidays with special food.

Lanterns

Set up a paper lantern craft on your craft table or other space. Look online for instructions, or make the classic fold-in-half-and-cut-slits model. You'll need construction paper, scissors, and tape. Gold and silver star stickers add a bright touch.

String your finished lanterns on a garland or hang them on a mobile. Traditional Eid colors are bright and cheerful and include a lot of green.

Fact challenge

Display books like these to support a Muslim History Fact Challenge or My Inspiration prompt.

Try these nonfiction titles:

Becoming Kareem: Growing Up On and Off the Court by Kareem Abdul-Jabbar

The Genius of Islam: How Muslims Made the Modern World by Bryn Barnard

Muslim Girls Rise: Inspirational Champions of Our Time by Saira Mir, Aaliya Jaleel

Proud (Young Readers Edition): Living My American Dream by Ibtihaj Muhammad

Malcolm Little: The Boy Who Grew Up to Become Malcolm X by Ilyasah Shabazz

1001 Inventions and Awesome Facts from Muslim Civilization by National Geographic

Twelve Rounds to Glory (12 Rounds to Glory): The Story of Muhammad Ali by Charles R. Smith Jr

Malala's Magic Pencil by Malala Yousafzai and Kerascoët

Say Hi

Say Hi is perfect for Ramadan, because not only do Muslim people speak many different languages, but even Arabic speakers may say "hello" in different ways, depending on where they are from and, in some cases, who they are talking to.

TABLE 9.6

Language	Spelling	Pronunciation
Egyptian Arabic	سلام عليكم	salām 'alaykum
Moghrebi Arabic (Morocco, Tunisia, Algeria)	السلام عليكم	Saalam uwaleekum
Turkish	Merhaba	
Tagalog	Kamusta	
Hausa	Sannu	
Hindi	नमस्कार	namaskaar
Pashto	سلام دي وي	Salaam alaikum
Persian (Farsi)	سلام	*Salām!*
Malay	Selamat pagi	Selamat pag-ee
Somali	Salaam alaykum	
Kurdish	Merheba!	
Bengali (Bangla)	আসসালামু আলাইকুম	**Assalamu Alaikum**
Albanian	Përshëndetje!	
Azerbaijani	Salam	
French	Bon jour	
Mandinka	Salaam aleikum	

Write your name

How does your name look transliterated into Arabic? How about Hindi, Pashto, Uighur, Mandarin, Javanese script, Bangla, or Farsi?

Booklist for Eid

For kids:

> *Once Upon an Eid: Stories of Hope and Joy by 15 Muslim Voices* edited by S. K. Ali
> *Lailah's Lunchbox* by Reem Faruqi
> *Meet Yasmin!* by Saadi Faruqi and Hatem Aly
> *Yo Soy Muslim: A Father's Letter to His Daughter* by Mark Gonzalez

My Grandma and Me by Mina Javaherbin, Lindsey Yankey
Golden Domes and Silver Lanterns by Hena Khan
Night of the Moon by Hena Khan
Amina's Voice by Hena Khan
Peg + Cat: The Eid al-Adha Adventure by Jennifer Oxley
The Proudest Blue by Ibtihaj Muhammad
Sadiq and the Desert Star by Siman Nuurali
Bilal Cooks Daal by Aisha Saeed
Other Words for Home by Jasmine Warga

For teens:

Does My Head Look Big in This? by Randa Abdel-Fattah
Mad, Bad, and Dangerous to Know by Samira Ahmed
Love from A to Z by S. K. Ali
A Girl Like That by Tanaz Bhathena
All-American Muslim Girl by Nadine Jolie Courtney
Here to Stay by Sara Farizan
Zara Hossain Is Here by Sabina Khan
A Very Large Expanse of Sea by Tahereh Mafi
Amal Unbound by Aisha Saeed

Asian Pacific Heritage Month

Put up an ID Challenge, a Find the Famous Folks scavenger hunt, or a My Inspiration prompt (see the beginning of this chapter).

You might include:

TABLE 9.7

Yo-Yo Ma	Musician
Dwayne The Rock Johnson	Actor and wrestler
Yayoi Kusuma	Artist
Marie Kondo	Household organizer
Tammy Duckworth	U.S. Senator, veteran
Duke Kahanamoku	Olympic swimmer, Surfer
Naomi Osaka	Tennis player, won the U.S. Open at the age of 21
Dr. Feng Shan Ho	Diplomat, Holocaust hero
Dalip Singh Saund	First Asian elected to Congress
Steven Chu	Nobel Prize–winning physicist
Maya Lin	Architect

(continued)

TABLE 9.7 (*Continued*)

Michelle Kwan	Figure skater with two Olympic medals and nine U.S. championships
Mazie Hirono	First Asian American woman elected to the Senate
Andrew Yang	Tech entrepreneur, 2019 Presidential candidate
Troy Polamalu	Football player, 2 Super Bowls, 2010 Defensive Player of the Year

Create your Manga identity

Here's a variation on a naming meme that is a little more elaborate. Set it up in a series of jars, one for each category, loaded with slips printed with that category's options. No need to take up a lot of desk space with Big Jars—recycled peanut butter jars or Mason jars do nicely for this challenge.

Or make this a table activity—type up the categories and options, numbering the options. Place the sheet in a sign holder and put out a big die or bowl of dice. Customers roll to find out what kind of manga character they will be. If you've got the skills to fold a four-part paper fortune teller (sometimes called a cootie catcher), you could use one of those for this passive program instead of a die.

TABLE 9.8

Will your character be a	Living in
Boy	A magic world
Girl	Space
Animal	The current real world
Robot	The past
Supernatural entity	Postapocalyptic world
Superhero	A world of animals

TABLE 9.9

I change shape when	I change into
I see the moon	A monster
I get really angry	An animal
I eat shrimp	A robot
I get wet	A different gender
I fall in love	A demon
Someone says a magic word	A vehicle

Supply this activity with drawing sheets or comic pages, and suggest that players draw their character, give them a name, and supply details. What kind of animal do you metamorphose into? What's your hair like?

Teru teru bōzu doll craft

A teru teru bōzu (shine shine monk) is a traditional handmade doll used to wish for good weather. Hang yours right-side-up to bring sunshine, or upside down to make it rain. Put out large squares of white tissue paper, lengths of yarn or string, and markers along with directions:

- Ball up one piece of tissue paper, place the ball in the center of a second piece.
- Gather the second piece of tissue around the ball to make a ghost shape.
- Tie the string or yarn around the paper underneath the wrapped ball.
- Draw a face!

Draw your Japanese family crest

Japanese heraldry symbols are usually circular. This makes it easy to provide blank crests for people to create a family badge. Cut out rounds of construction paper, or put out jar lids as templates. Print a selection of Japanese heraldic symbols (easy to find on the Internet) for design inspiration.

Your art supplies should include markers in deep, strong colors, as well as gold and silver if possible.

Asian Pacific American booklist

Krista Kim-Bap by Angela Ahn

We Are Not Free by Traci Chee

Drum Dream Girl: How One Girl's Courage Changed Music by Margarita Engle and Rafael López

Gaijin: American Prisoner of War by Matt Faulkner

Hoʻonani: Hula Warrior by Heather Gale and Mika Song

Red Kite, Blue Kite by Ji-li Jiang, Greg Ruth

At Home in Her Tomb: Lady Dai and the Ancient Chinese Treasures of Mawangdui by Christine Liu-Perkins

It Began with a Page: How Gyo Fujikawa Drew the Way by Kyo Maclear and Julie Morstad

Barbed Wire Baseball by Marissa Moss, Yuko Shimizu

Priya Dreams of Marigolds & Masala by Meenal Patel

Yayoi Kusama: From Here to Infinity by Sarah Suzuki, Ellen Weinstein

They Called Us Enemy by George Takei, Justin Eisinger, Steven Scott, and Harmony Becker

Natsumi's Song of Summer by Robert Paul Weston and Misa Saburi
Ten Cents a Pound by Nhung N. Tran-Davies
The Shadow Hero by Gene Luen Yang, Sonny Liew
Amy Wu and the Perfect Bao by Kat Zhang and Charlene Chua

Summer

Book recommendations

Summer is a great time for book recommendations. Solicit beach reads, memoirs, steamy summer lovin', or "cool off with a hot title" recommendations on your whiteboard, bulletin board, mobile, garland, or chalkboard.

Some great summer stories to get the wheels turning

For kids:

Be Prepared by Vera Brosgol
Camp Tiger by Susan Choi
Jabari Jumps by Gaia Cornwall
Dead End in Norvelt by Jack Gantos
One Crazy Summer by Rita Williams Garcia
The Parker Inheritance by Varian Johnson
All Summer Long by Hope Larson
As Brave as You by Jason Reynolds

For teens and adults, populate a display with books by Nancy Thayer, Elin Hilderbrand, Mary Kay Andrews, and Joshilyn Jackson.

Record highs

Challenge library customers to match geographic locations to the record high temperatures recorded there. Death Valley (201 degrees), Sudan (183.2)—but also Esperanza Base, Antarctica (63.5 degrees) and Arkhangelsk, Russia (84 degrees—pretty hot for a city north of the Arctic Circle!). Don't forget your hometown—Baltimore, Maryland, hit 107 degrees in 1936! See the Appendix for online sources of historic weather data.

Summer reading

When planning your summer reading programming, be sure to incorporate lots of passive programs. Take advantage of visits from day camps and day care centers, and have lots of quick crafts and pencil puzzles on hand for kids to do while you are busy signing them all up for your summer program.

Broad themes like music, space, ocean life, and so on can easily be adapted to passive programs that will promote the theme throughout your branch or system and lead to increased SR enthusiasm and participation.

Series books like the Lots to Spot series and Puzzle it Out from Windmill Press are packed with themed reproducible puzzles that you can pass out in a hurry even when you're taken by surprise. Be sure to find a page that fits your summer reading theme!

June

My summer goals

Write or draw your plans for the summer. Will you read ten books? Learn to dive? Solve a mystery? This works on a whiteboard or a chalkboard, but you'll elicit interesting stories if you put out blank comic book creation paper.

PRIDE

Stock your craft table with every kind of rainbow craft you can think up. Be extra inclusive by showing off the Philadelphia Pride flag, which includes black and brown stripes, as your example. Any Pride program should be accompanied by related books, movies, and a list of support resources, including websites and hotline numbers.

Clothesline for Pride

Use twine, yarn, or actual clothesline rope to create a clothesline on a wall, bulletin board or in a window. Set out T-shirts, handkerchiefs, or fabric squares along with glitter glue, fabric markers, puffy paint, or other materials that work well on cloth.

Customers are asked to decorate the object using the prompt "what Pride means to me" for inspiration. Hang their creation on the line with clips or clothespins.

Button making

Pride month is another great time to break out your button maker if you have one. Print Pride slogans, use rainbow wrapping paper, or let customers design their own button blanks.

Rainbow book stacks

Make your June scavenger hunt a celebration of Pride! Challenge customers to find a book with a red spine, an orange spine, yellow, green, and so on. Successful spectrum sleuths can present their literary rainbow to you for a prize or add it to a display. Either way, use these stacks of colorful books to create a giant tower, display, or shelf, and don't forget to take a picture before reshelving!

Juneteenth

Make June 19 a day of celebration of history, pride, and beauty. Borrow activities from Black History Month (February), especially a story quilt craft.

Collage board

Give your bulletin board or wall a nice big title, "Juneteenth," and a paragraph describing the significance of the day. Provide collage materials like old magazines, and prompt visitors to find images that they associate with emancipation, Black history, or celebration which they can then add to your big Juneteenth collage.

Great books to display on Juneteenth

> *Crown* by Derrick Barnes
> *Freedom over Me: Eleven Slaves, Their Lives and Dreams Brought to Life* by Ashley Bryan
> *Hair Love* by Matthew A. Cherry
> *Juneteenth for Mazie* by Floyd Cooper
> *Hands Up!* by Breanna J. McDaniel and Shane W. Evans
> *All Different Now: Juneteenth, the First Day of Freedom* by Angela Johnson
> *Black Is a Rainbow Color* by Angela Joy
> *Juneteenth* by Vaunda Micheaux Nelson
> *Freedom in Congo Square* by Carole Boston Weatherford
> *Freedom's Gifts* by Valerie Wilson Wesley

July

What America means to me

Here's a writing prompt that really gets to the heart of your customers' values. Post the responses on a map of the United States or a big drawing of the American flag. Be sure to take a lot of pictures of the answers—this can be used to prompt discussion during other programs or even during staff meetings. Pro tip: Don't use a real flag; someone is bound to complain.

Born on the 4th of July booklist:

> Action Presidents! series
> *V is for Voting* by Karen Farrell
> *Blue Sky White Stars* by Sarvinder Naberhaus

Of Thee I Sing: A Letter to My Daughters by Barack Obama

Her Right Foot by Dave Eggers

Around America to Win the Vote: Two Suffragists, a Kitten, and 10,000 Miles by Mara Rockliff

Ida B. Wells: Let the Truth Be Told by Walter Dean Myers

Founding Mothers: Remembering the Ladies by Cokie Roberts

When You Grow Up to Vote by Eleanor Roosevelt

American heroes scavenger hunt

Midway through the summer is a fine time for a few history games. Put together an ID Challenge, a Find the Folks scavenger hunt, and especially a My Inspiration board. Be sure that your list of U.S. heroes goes beyond the founding fathers, and includes plenty of people of color, Indigenous people, and women.

You'll find these folks on the best scavenger hunts:

Shirley Chisolm

Tammy Duckworth

Joy Harjo

Jane Jacobs

Mae Jemison

Katherine Johnson

Barbara Jordan

John Lewis

Thurgood Marshall

Barbara Mikulski

Sally Ride

Bayard Rustin

Elizabeth Cady Stanton

Margaret Sanger

Sequoyah

August

Trung Thu—Children's Festival (Vietnam)

Tet-Trung-Thu is celebrated on August 15. This festival is all about children, with an emphasis on school success, which ties in nicely with back-to-school activities and themes.

Trung Thu is celebrated with masks and star-shaped lanterns—set up supplies on your craft table and encourage customers to make a mask or lantern to take home and one to decorate the library.

Back to School

If my teacher weren't a teacher, they'd be. . . .

This is a terrific writing and/or drawing prompt in the children's department.

My weird school

Celebrate Dan Gutman's silly chapter book series with this vocabulary-stretching wordplay prompt. Let your library customers come up with titles for new books in the series based on the names of library staff.

Sure, *Ms. Willey is Silly* is a no-brainer, but *Ms. Amaral is* . . . ? This challenge is harder than it sounds (hint: Ms. Amaral is a real pal)!

Write "Ms. YourNameHere is ____" on your whiteboard or chalkboard with plenty of room for participants to add adjectives that rhyme with the name. Keep an eagle eye on this one in case some smarty-pants interprets this prompt as an invitation to rudeness.

Or print these fill-in-the-blank prompts on slips for customers to fill out with their suggestions and drop in a jar or entry box. Winner to be drawn at random, best answers to be printed out and worn as a nametag for a week!

New school supplies

Set this up as a poll or a writing/drawing prompt. What's your favorite school supply? A spanking clean new notebook? Or a funky new pencil case? Paradoxically, this goes over better with adults. For some reason, kids just aren't as jazzed about brand-new pens and pencils as we grownups are.

My favorite class

A classic poll question for a whiteboard or bulletin board. You can add "recess" or "none of the above" to the options, but younger kids will usually answer this question sincerely. If you're good at math, that's your favorite class!

Autumn

Book to art—Leaf Man

Lois Ehlert often includes activities in the back of her colorful, collage-y picture books, and her classic *Leaf Man* is no exception. If you live in an area where trees drop their leaves in the fall, organize a leaf hunt, and then put the fallen leaves in a basket on the craft table. Provide markers and glue and showcase pages from the book (color copies are better than the real thing).

Take pictures of the resulting leaf collages before they leave the library and display them on a board or on the library's social media.

September

Hispanic Heritage Month

Hispanic Heritage Month runs from September 15 to October 15. Because it celebrates places as well as people, this month lends itself to people-focused passive programs like ID Challenge, Find the Folks, and My Inspiration as well as Fact Challenges.

Say Hi

Level up your Say Hi challenge by including native languages like Quechua, Guarani, and Aymara. We'll make it easy – Hello, how are you is "Allian-chu" (pronounced Eye-eee-anch-ooo) in Quechua. In Guarani, "Mbaẽichapa reiko?" means how are you. And in Aymara, hello is the cheerful "Laphi!"

Find the Folks

Steal this list of notable Latinx and Chicanx people for your egg hunt, ID Challenge, or Find the Famous Folks:

TABLE 9.10

Sonia Sotomayor	First Latinx woman appointed to the U.S. Supreme Court
Jennifer Lopez	Ultra-famous Latinx singer and actress
Cesar Chavez	Labor leader
Elizabeth Acevedo	Afro-Dominican author and poet who won the National Book Award for Young People for her first novel, *The Poet X*
Pablo Casals	World-famous cello player
Frida Kahlo	Painter famous for her self-portraits and paintings of animals
Ellen Ochoa	First Latinx woman in space
Carlos Juan Finlay	Cuban doctor who discovered that mosquitos spread yellow fever
Julián Castro	Former Secretary of Housing and Urban Development and Democratic presidential candidate in 2019
Idelisa Bonnelly	The "mother of marine conservation in the Caribbean," founded the Dominican Foundation for Marine Research and the Institute for Marine Biology

(continued)

TABLE 9.10 (*Continued*)

Dr. Helen Rodriguez Trías (1929–2001)	Founded the first center for newborn children in Puerto Rico; AIDS/HIV activist who was elected the first Latina president of the American Public Health Association
Mario Molina, Chemist, Scientist (1943–)	Won a Nobel Prize in 1995 for research on how manmade compounds affect the ozone layer
Laura I. Gomez	Founding member of Twitter international
Nicole Hernandez Hammer	Climate science and community advocate at the Union of Concerned Scientists
Stephanie Castillo	Founder of Latina Girls Code, which sponsors workshops and hackathons to teach Latina girls computer and entrepreneurial skills
Nydia Velázquez	First Puerto Rican woman to serve in the U.S. Congress
Hilda Lucia Solis	Former Secretary of Labor and U.S. Congresswoman
Alexandria Ocasio-Cortez	Aka AOC, an American politician and activist who serves as the U.S. Representative for New York's 14th congressional district

Find books that represent the diversity of Latinx culture.
For kids:

Planting Stories: The Life of Librarian and Storyteller Pura Belpré by Anika
    Aldamuy Denise
Dancing Hands: How Teresa Carreño Played the Piano for President Lincoln by
    Margarita Engle
Bravo!: Poems about Amazing Hispanics by Margarita Engle
Yo Soy Muslim: A Father's Letter to His Daughter by Mark Gonzalez
Ada's Violin: The Story of the Recycled Orchestra of Paraguay by Susan Hood
Martí's Song for Freedom/Martí y sus versos por la libertad by Emma Otheguy
My Papi Has a Motorcycle by Isabel Quintero
Dreamers by Yuyi Morales

For teens:

Tales from la Vida edited by Frederick Luis Aldama
Brooklyn Brujas (trilogy) Zoraida Cordova
Shadowshaper (trilogy) by Daniel Jose Older
Juliet Takes a Breath by Gabby Rivera
Aristotle and Dante Discover the Secrets of the Universe by Benjamin Alire Sáenz
I Am Not Your Perfect Mexican Daughter by Erika Sanchez
*The Other Side: Stories of Central American Teen Refugees Who Dream of
    Crossing the Border* by Juan Pablo Villalobos

For adults:

Fruit of the Drunken Tree by Ingrid Rojas Contreras
Cantoras by Carolina de Robertis
The Book of Unknown Americans by Cristina Henríquez
The Beast: Riding the Rails and Dodging Narcos on the Migrant Trail by Óscar
   Martínez
Puerto Rico Strong edited by Hazel Newlevant
Forgotten Continent: A History of the New Latin America by Michael Reid

Banned Books Week

Match game

Take the Banned Books Week Match Game Quiz! See if you can match these books with the reasons people stated as why they should be banned! Bonus question: in which cases do you think the stated reason was the complainant's actual problem with the book? (See: *Persepolis* by Marjane Satrapi, banned for its "depiction of gambling.")

TABLE 9.11

Challenged or banned book	Stated reason
1. *Kite Runner* by Khaled Hosseini	A. Offensive language
2. *It's So Amazing* by Robie Harris	B. Sex education
3. *Looking for Alaska* by John Green	C. Offensive language
4. *The Perks of Being a Wallflower* by Stephen Chbosky	D. Alcohol
5. *Two Boys Kissing* by David Levithan	E. Homosexuality
6. *The Bluest Eye* by Toni Morrison	F. Contains controversial issues
7. *Habibi* by Craig Thompson	G. Nudity
8. *Drama* by Raina Telgemeier	H. Sexually explicit
9. *Persepolis* by Marjane Satrapi	I. Gambling
10. *The Hate U Give* by Angie Thomas	J. "anti-cop"

Banned Books popularity contest

Post ALA's list of most frequently challenged books as a poll. Vote using your Big Jar or make hashmarks on a whiteboard or bulletin board. Spoiler: Harry Potter will win every time.

Banned Book in a Jar

When a popular book that is on the frequently challenged list is weeded for condition, use a paper cutter to cut its pages into strips ½–1" wide. Keep these in a labeled zip-top bag until Banned Book Week comes around; then load them into a jar. Post a list of the most frequently challenged titles next to your jar, making it easier for customers to figure out which book is inside (and raising awareness of censorship in the bargain). Reward every correct answer or provide an Enter to Win box.

Be sure you make it *very clear* that the library discarded this book for condition, and that you have more copies on the shelf! You do not want this to backfire into an assumption that the library is destroying controversial content. Andria's library avoids this issue entirely by copying significant passages of the book from online sites and pasting them into a Word document, which they cut into strips to fill the jar. If you do this, you can load the center of the jar with crumpled pieces of scrap paper and just make enough printed pieces to create visible outer layer.

International Talk Like a Pirate Day (September 19)

What be ye pirate name? Post correlation lists or create a meme, e.g.: color of your shirt + favorite game + "the Pirate." Arrr! I be Black Plaid Scrabble the Pirate!

Tip: Don't use "color of ye shirt" if lots of your kid customers wear school uniforms. You'll end up with fifty scurvy scallywags named "Dark Green Fortnight the Pirate."

TABLE 9.12

Month ye were born	Piratical first name
January	Pegleg
February	Blind
March	Stinky
April	Bloody
May	Mad
June	Could-Use-a-Shave
July	Seriously Unpleasant
August	Captain
September	Two-Toed
October	Black-Hearted
November	Pottymouth
December	Sharkbait

TABLE 9.13

Color of ye socks	Pirate last name
Red	Bart
Orange	Prince Albert
Yellow	Barnacle Jack
Green	Johnny Crablegs
Blue	Commodore Charlie
Purple	Jasmine the Bonecrusher
Brown	Ruthless Maria
Black	Pete
White	Jared
Multi	Crustyshorts Carla

October

Korean National Foundation Day

National Foundation Day (Kae Chun Jul) celebrates the founding of Korea in 2333 BCE. See the beginning of this chapter for instructions on how to put up a Fact Challenge, Say Hi, or Write Your Name in Hangul.

How to bow

Play YouTube videos showing the proper way to execute a Korean bow. Anyone who bows to a member of library staff gets a prize.

K-Pop challenge

Korean pop groups come and go pretty quickly, but when they're hot they're everywhere. Make a match game pairing performers with their groups. Or make it a poll—Girls Generation or Blackpink? Best hair in K-Pop? Who's your favorite member of BTS?

Korean inspirations booklist:

The Ocean Calls by Tina Cho
The Name Jar by Yangsook Choi
Bee-Bim Bop! by Linda Sue Park
No Kimchi for Me! By Aram Kim
Where's Halmoni? by Julie Kim
The Turtle Ship by Helena Ku Rhee

Star Wars Reads Day

Star Wars was made for trivia quizzes and match games. Here are just a couple.

Planet match

TABLE 9.14

Star Wars planet	Description
1. Coruscant	A. Governmental center of the Republic and later the Empire
2. Endor	B. Where the Ewoks live
3. Tatooine	C. Where Luke grew up
4. Jakku	D. Where Rey is from
5. Hoth	E. Ice planet with Tauntauns
6. Ahch-To	F. Luke's retirement planet
7. Kashyyyk	G. Wookiee homeworld
8. Alderaan	H. Leia's home planet; very blown up
9. Takodana	I. Maz Kanata lives here
10. Crait	J. Ice planet with crystal foxes (vulptexes)
11. Scarif	K. Tropical planet, Galactic Empire research and development facility
12. Kessel	L. Impoverished desert planet fought over by crime lords because of valuable natural resources (spice and hyperfuel)

Star Wars word scramble

Use the names of the planets listed above and scramble them for young Jedis to decipher.

Lightsaber color match

Here's an easy one—match the Jedi and Sith masters to the colors of their lightsaber blades. Luke's is blue (at first), Yoda's is green, and Kylo Ren wields a ridiculous red broadsword lightsaber, but only Samuel L. Jackson's Mace Windu got a purple lightsaber.

There are literally thousands of Star Wars crafts and activities in books and online; we have faith in your ability to find the droids you're looking for.

Diwali

Diwali is the Hindu festival of lights celebrated every autumn. It signifies the victory of light over dark, good over evil, and knowledge over ignorance. Perfect for the library!

Super-safe "oil" lamps

Small clay oil lamps are a traditional symbol of Diwali. Here's a way to let your customers make one to decorate the library while they learn about this holiday.

Collect plastic water bottles. Cut across the bottles (easy to do with regular scissors) about two inches from the bottom, so that you have a little cup. Set these out along with brown, black, and yellow permanent markers or paint pens. Customers will color the cup all over with brown marker and then add decorations in the other colors.

Add a battery-powered votive candle and put the lamp in a window or on a display.

Henna hand

Stock your craft table with construction paper and markers, along with printouts of lots of different types of mehndi designs. Invite library users to trace around their own hand and then decorate their hand shape with lacy geometric designs, curlicues, and dots. Do a google image search on "mehndi template" for a wide selection of beautiful designs.

If they can bear to leave their beautiful creation in the library, make a garland of waving, welcoming hands.

South Asian Muslims also apply mehndi during Eid (May), so this is a lovely craft to put out during those festivals, too.

Indigenous Peoples' Day

Also called First Peoples' Day or Columbus Day in some areas, Indigenous Peoples' Day is a holiday that celebrates and honors Native American peoples and commemorates their histories and cultures. It falls on the second Monday in October.

Get a jump-start on Native American Heritage Month (November) and raise awareness of the decolonization of this holiday with passive programming. Try a Fact Challenge or Say Hi, or one of the match games listed under Native American Heritage Month.

Halloween

Scare the librarian

Find a library staff member and tell them the scariest story you can think of! Post this challenge on your whiteboard, chalkboard, bulletin board or display. Make sure your staff doesn't spook easily first!

Pick a monster

Fill your Big Jar with words or pictures of werewolves, vampires, ghosts, and zombies. Customers pick a slip and then must find a book or movie that features such a creature. Make it easy for your kid customers with a display featuring Goosebumps books, Monster High, Scary Stories to Tell in the Dark, and more.

Passport program: Read your way through the Monster Pantheon

Can you read one book about each type of monster?

FOR KIDS

A display full of Unicorn Rescue Society or books from the Hazy Dell Press Monster Series will inspire their monstrous reading.

Aliens: *We're Not from Here* by Geoff Rodkey
Chupacabras: *El Chupacabras* by Adam Rubin
Djinn: *The Amulet of Samarkand* by Jonathan Stroud
Ghost: *Leo* by Mac Barnett
Sasquatch: *Larf* by Ashley Spires
Scary mermaid: Jumbies series by Tracy Baptiste
Sea monster: *Nessie Quest* by Melissa Savage
Vampire: *Vampirina Ballerina* by Ann Marie Pace
Zombie: *Peanut Butter and Brains* by Joe McGee

IN THE TEEN SECTION

Aliens: *Adaptation* by Malinda Lo
Djinn/Ifrit: *Raybearer* by Jordan Ifueko

Genetically engineered plague: *Wilder Girls* by Rory Power
Ghost: *A Long Way Down* by Jason Reynolds
Scary mermaids: *The Vicious Deep* by Zoraida Córdova
Sea monster: *Salt* by Hannah Moskowitz
Serial killer: *Burn Baby Burn* by Meg Medina
Vampire: *The Beautiful* by Renee Ahdieh
Werewolf: *Out of Salem* by Hal Schrieve
Zombies: *Last Ones Left Alive* by Sarah Davis-Goff

FOR ADULTS

Aliens: *The Seep* by Chana Porter
Djinn: *City of Brass* by S. A. Chakraborty
Genetically engineered tapeworm: *The Troop* by Nick Cutter
Ghost: *The Book of Lost Saints* by Daniel Jose Older
Scary mermaids: *Into the Drowning Deep* by Mira Grant
Sea monster: *The Scar* by China Miéville
Serial killer: *Heartsick* by Chelsea Cain
Vampire: *Certain Dark Things* by Silvia Moreno-Garcia
Werewolf: *The Last Werewolf* by Glen Duncan
Zombies: *Boneshaker* by Cherie Priest

Make a monster

For this one you need two Big Jars (or boxes). Print pictures of scary specimens and then cut them in half crosswise. Put the top halves in one jar and the bottoms in the other. Customers pick a top and a bottom and then have to make up a name and description for the chimerical creep they've produced. What's scarier—a vampwolf? Or a zombacabra?

Post these horrific hybrids on a board or wall along with their made-up names and descriptions.

What scares you?

Invite customers to write or draw their deepest (or their silliest) fear and drop it into the safe anonymity of the Big Jar. This works on a board, mobile, or garland as well, of courseIbut the Jar never tells and never pokes fun.

Recommendation prompt: What's the last book you read (or movie your watched) that totally creeped you out?

This prompt is a perennial favorite. For some reasons, super-scary books and movies stick in people's minds. Leverage your customers' responses into a

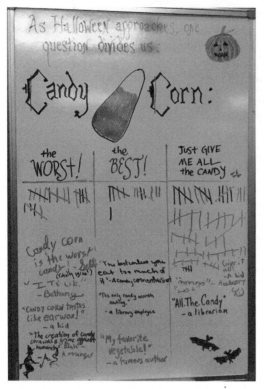

The most divisive question ever to appear on Paula's whiteboard: Candy corn: Yuck? or Yum?

great list or display—Books/Movies That Freaked Out Your Neighbors.

Recommendation prompt: What do you read (or watch) when you are upset?

The flip side to Halloween scares—what books or other media do we use to self-soothe? Pair this with a display of cozy mysteries, childhood classics like Anne of Green Gables, or DVDs of *The Great British Baking Show*.

Vote

Candy corn

Yum? Yuck? Or "Just give me all the candy"? Every year, this is the most divisive poll question ever to appear on Paula's whiteboard. Friendships are forged or broken over the candy corn conundrum. Even your authors, who agree on nearly everything, are on opposite sides of this debate (Paula says "yum," and Andria says "candy corn is scarier than zombies.")

November

Native American Heritage Month

Celebrating the native cultures of North America is eye-opening and can be a lot of fun. Try doing a Fact Challenge, ID Challenge, Find the Folks, Say Hi (there are a lot of languages to choose from!), and Write Your Name. See the appendix for online resources about native languages and alphabets.

Look online for activities recommended by First Nation people in order to avoid cultural appropriation or perpetuation of stereotypes.

Find the folks

Prominent people of Native American heritage:

TABLE 9.15

Chief Joseph (Nez Perce)	Chief and humanitarian
Geronimo (Chiricahua Apache)	Leader and fighter
Wilma Mankiller (Cherokee)	Activist, social worker, community developer and the first woman elected Principal Chief of the Cherokee Nation
Sharice Davids (Ho-Chunk)	U.S. Representative from Kansas 3rd District, 2019–Present
Deb Haaland (Laguna Pueblo)	U.S. Representative from New Mexico 1st District, 2019–Present
Joseph Bruchac (Abenaki)	Author and poet, author of *Code Talker: A Novel About the Navajo Marines of World War Two* and *Skeleton Man*
Louise Erdrich (Turtle Mountain Ojibwe)	Author, poet, author of *The Round House* and *Love Medicine*
Joy Harjo (Muscogee Creek Nation-Cherokee)	Poet Laureate of the United States
Taboo (Shoshone descent)	Rapper, member of the Black Eyed Peas
Will Rogers (Cherokee)	Humorist and actor
Louis Sockalexis (Penobscot)	Major league baseball player
Jim Thorpe (Sac and Fox Nation)	Olympic gold medalist, pentathlon and decathlon, professional baseball, football and basketball player
Elizabeth Jean Peratrovich (Tlingit)	Civil rights activist instrumental in the passage of Alaska's Anti-Discrimination Act of 1945
Sacajawea (Shoshone)	Translator, member of the Lewis and Clark Expedition
Sequoyah (Cherokee)	Inventor of the Cherokee syllabary
Ishi (Yahi)	Last surviving Yahi
Maria Tallchief (Osage Nation)	America's first prima ballerina
John Herrington (Chickasaw Nation)	Astronaut, on the space shuttle and International Space Station. First enrolled member of a Native American tribe to fly in space.
David Archambault II (Lakota)	Former tribal chair of Standing Rock Indian Reservation, a leader of the Dakota Access Pipeline protests in 2016

Say Hi

TABLE 9.16

Language	Greeting
Cherokee	O'-Si-Yo'
Lakota/Dakota Sioux	Hau
Yucatec Mayan	Ba'ax ka wa'alik?
Dene Navajo	Ya'at'eeh
Yupik Eskimo	Apaa
Alutiiq	Cama'i (Cha-My)
Chickasaw	Hallito
Mahican	Koonumunthe
Micosukkee (Seminole)	Che-hen-ta-mo?
Ojibwe (Chippewa)	Boozhoo
Hawaiian	Aloha
Unagax (Aleut)	Aang (Pronounce like "song")

Sources: American Indian Alaska Native Tourism Association, https://www.aianta.org/words-of-welcome/ and PowWows.com

Story quilt

Some Native American cultures use quilts to tell stories. See Chapter 7 for a great craft table quilt activity.

Match game

Lists of place names that derive from Native words are easy to find online. Make a match game between the current names and their original meanings.

Passport program: Decolonize your reading

In the past, Native American stories were often written by people who were not Native. Challenge your library customers to read their way through a batch of #ownvoices literature to win a special prize. We've listed a good sampling of titles in various genres below—for an extra challenge, ask readers to sample books written by authors with a variety of tribal affiliations.

The American Indian Youth Literature Award winner lists can offer helpful suggestions. Here are some of our favorites:

nattiq and the Land of Statues: A Story from the Arctic by Barbara Landry
We Are Water Protectors by Carole Lindstrom
Bowwow Powwow by Brenda J. Child

SkySisters by Jan Bourdeau Waboose

I Am Not a Number by Dr. Jenny Kay Dupuis

We Are Grateful: Otsaliheliga by Traci Sorrell

At the Mountain's Base by Traci Sorell

When We Were Alone by David A. Robertson

Encounter by Brittany Luby

Fry Bread by Kevin Noble Maillard

First Laugh Welcome Baby by Rose Ann Tahe, Nancy Bo Flood, and Jonathan Nelson

Wilma's Way Home: The Life of Wilma Mankiller by Doreen Rappaport

For teens and adults:

History: *An Indigenous Peoples' History of the United States* by Roxanne Dunbar-Ortiz

Memoir: *Crazy Brave* by Joy Harjo

Essays: *Abandon Me* by Melissa Febos

Anthology: *#NotYourPrincess* edited by Lisa Charleyboy and Mary Beth Leatherdale

Literary fiction: *There There* by Tommy Orange

Crime fiction: *The Round House* by Louise Erdrich

Horror: *Mapping the Interior* by Stephen Graham Jones

Fantasy: *Trail of Lightning* by Rebecca Roanhorse

YA fiction: *Hearts Unbroken* by Cynthia Leitich Smith

Dia de los Muertos (November 2)

Dia de los Muertos is celebrated throughout Mexico, Central America, and parts of South America. In Ecuador it's called Dia de los Difuntos (deceased) and in Bolivia it's Dia de los Natitos (skulls). Pay attention to your library's demographics and do some research on Day of the Dead traditions pertinent to the people in your area. It is always good to partner with a community group if nobody on your staff is in touch with their Central or South American heritage.

Ofrenda

Ofrenda is an altar commemorating friends and family who have passed away. It can be an elaborate floor-mounted construction or a tiny table display. You could even fit one on an empty shelf. Marigolds and candles often appear on ofrendas alongside favorite foods and pictures of the deceased.

Invite your customers to contribute memorials to their own loved ones. Ask them to draw or print out a picture of a loved one or respected figure who has died. They can draw in foods that person liked, pets they owned, or symbols of their accomplishments.

Masks

Stock your craft table with blank cardboard masks and examples of calaveras for inspiration. Hang completed masks on your mobile, post them on your bulletin board, or use them to decorate a display of seasonal materials – if you can convince your customers to leave them!

Books by Latinx artists will provide design inspiration. Here are just a few:

Pablo Remembers by George Ancona
Day of the Dead by Tony Johnston and Jeanette Winter
Clatter Bash! A Day of the Dead Celebration by Richard Keep
Just a Minute: A Trickster Tale & Counting Book by Yuyi Morales
Dia de Los Muertos by Roseanne Greenfield Thong
Funny Bones: Posada and His Day of the Dead Calaveras by Duncan Tonatiuh
Calavera Abecedario: A Day of the Dead Alphabet Book by Jeanette Winter

Election Day

Writing/art prompt

Add a little humor to the democratic process with a prompt that asks, "What fictional character would you vote for to be President? Vice President?" At Paula's branch, we saw responses ranging from Curious George to Walter White from *Breaking Bad*! For the record, Walter White would be a *terrible* president.

Your election day display could include the following:

Sofia Valdez, Future Prez by Andrea Beaty and David Roberts
Equality's Call: The Story of Voting Rights in America by Deborah Diesen, illustrated by Magdalena Mora
Grace Goes to Washington by Kelly DiPucchio, LeUyen Pham
Votes of Confidence: A Young Person's Guide to American Elections by Jeff Fleischer
The Next President: The Unexpected Beginnings and Unwritten Future of America's Presidents by Kate Messner, illustrated by Adam Rex
The President of the Jungle by André Rodrigues
Lillian's Right to Vote: A Celebration of the Voting Rights Act of 1965 by Jonah Winter

Thanksgiving

What are you thankful for?

On the craft table, provide brown paper, markers and scissors. Draw around your hand and cut it out. Write five things you're thankful for on the fingers and thumb. Add an eye and a beak, and look at that—you've got a turkey! Customers can take their turkey home or leave it at the library to make a gratefulness mobile or garland. Tack the turkeys to the front of your desk if there's no time to make a 3D display.

No craft table? "What are you thankful for?" is a lovely writing or drawing prompt for a whiteboard, chalkboard, or bulletin board.

Winter

Track match

If you live in an area that gets snow, winter is a great time for a match game featuring animal tracks. Print actual-size animal footprints and mount them on your board or wall alongside a list of the animals that made them.

How cold is cold?

Make a match game out of historically low temperatures and their locations. Vostok Station, Antarctica once dropped to $-128.6°F$ while the coldest temperature ever recorded on the continent of Africa was $-11°F$ in Morocco. Be sure to include local records!

See the Appendix for online weather records resources.

December

For the sake of inclusivity, celebrate the "holiday season," or "the season of giving."

Draw your favorite holiday treat

This whiteboard or chalkboard prompt always inspires delicious flights of fancy. You'll see giant gingerbread people, *pasteles* with mounds of icing, and sprinkles on everything.

Try this prompt on the craft table, and provide scissors, glue sticks, and construction paper along with markers and crayons. Add completed confections to a garland or mobile for a cheerful addition to your seasonal décor.

Book recommendations

Holidays are a great time to get a little reading in. Solicit cozy reads, steamy reads, heartwarming stories, or traditional tales on your whiteboard, garland, or mobile.

Give a book station

If you maintain a stash of Advance Reader Copies and leftover summer reading prize books, the holiday season is a great time to get those books into appreciative hands. Many kids (and adults) don't have a lot of opportunities or cash to shop for holiday gifts for family and friends. Set up a book cart or a table as a one-stop gift shop and wrapping station.

Provide all the gift wrap, wrapping supplies, and materials to make gift tags and cards. Or set up a Make Your Own Gift Wrap table. It's fun and easy to make wrapping paper out of large sheets of newsprint. Stamps and stamp pads are your not-too-messy friends for this craft.

Do this as a one-day event, or open your "free bookstore" on multiple days.

Tip: Document your success with this program and you might be able to get your wrapping supplies (or even books) donated by a local merchant next time you do it.

INSTANT REPLAY:

A boy approaches the desk, visibly shaken, Women's History trivia question crumpled in his fist.

Him: "I.....just... I just learned something..."

Me: "Did you find the answer to that question?"

Him: [nods slowly, stunned] "I always thought JK Rowling was a boy's name. But it's a GIRL. Her name is JOANNE.

Now I'm questioning everything I ever thought I knew."

10

Outside the Lines: The World Beyond Your Library

Library participation doesn't have to stop at the front door of your building. We challenge you to think outside the box of those four walls! Survey your library's surroundings and adapt our ideas to create interaction opportunities that inspire creativity, foster stewardship, and extend your reach into the community.

In this chapter you'll find indoor/outdoor passive programs that start at the craft table and extend to the library grounds, passive programs that are available to customers without even stepping foot in the library, and passive programs that will entice brand new users to come in through that front door and discover all you have to offer.

Use the trees, fencing or gardens around your library to display durable, customer-created artwork. Build civic pride and unity by offering self-guided community tours and neighborhood scavenger hunts with the library as home base. Create opportunities for people to look at themselves and the world around them in new and unexpected ways.

Some of these ideas may be harder to quantify for statistical purposes than others, but with a little extra thought and using the methods we've taught you so far, you can build in elements to assist with this goal. We believe in you.

On the library grounds

More and more libraries are incorporating beautiful green spaces into the design of new buildings. Whether you work in one of those or are surrounded by a concrete cityscape, there are ways to make the most of any outdoor areas around your building.

Colonizing your outdoor space gives you something constructive to offer kids and teens with physical energy to burn off and helps combat what has come to be called "nature deficit disorder," a term coined by Richard Louv, the founder of Children and Nature Network.

Refer back to the Nature Nook section of Chapter 8 and tweak those ideas into activities that send users outside to observe and appreciate the natural world, or try one of the following:

Plant life

Take and post pictures of the various trees, flowers, and plants that grow on the library grounds, and challenge customers to go outside and find them all. Make a checklist so they can mark things off as they locate them, and reward completed checklists with small prize or enter them into a raffle.

A garden of verses

Bring literature into your outdoor areas with a poetry garden. Laminate sheets of construction paper and cut them into flower shapes. Print a selection of your favorite short poems, laminate them, and glue or staple one to the center of each flower. Attach the flowers to dowels or stakes and plant them around your library's green space. Use one of the flowers to point users to the call number for poetry books. Add a weatherproof sign directing visitors to come inside and tell staff which poem they liked best to be entered in a raffle. Alternatively, encourage them to submit poems they have written or found in your collection to be added to the garden.

Don't have a garden or green space? You could line up flower pots or jars filled with sand along the library entrance and stick a poetry flower in each one.

Chalk challenges

If you have a sidewalk, concrete wall, or bit of pavement in a safe location on library property, use it to implement the drawing or writing prompts for whiteboards described in (or inspired by) this book. Set out a bucket of sidewalk chalk, and consider marking off the designated area with traffic cones, masking tape or another method to keep it contained to one area and prevent absent-minded passersby from bumping into the chalk artists at work.

Rock gardens

Painted rocks are a whole thing lately, in case you haven't noticed. Whether or not you have access to an outside space there are ways to use painted rocks for decoration and engagement. Even urban libraries with no green space can line up painted rocks outside the entrance, create a rock garden on a window ledge, or use them to spell out an encouraging word on the service desk.

Ask participants in library rock painting programs to paint an extra one for the library's rock garden. Or set up a craft table with rocks and paint pens in a common area, and invite all customers to decorate rocks and "plant" them in the garden. The next time they visit the library, they'll look for their creation and get a sense of ownership and pride when they find it.

Take your rock garden to the next level and encourage interaction and exploration by trying one of the following ideas. You may want to enlist coworkers to help with the prep work on these–maybe you can this activity to the agenda for your next staff in-service day or youth services meeting.

Library information

Remind passersby where they are and what they're missing with painted rocks that show the library's logo, Wi-Fi network name, and password. You know they're sitting outside using our Wi-Fi, why not let them know we're perfectly ok with it? Add a rock with the library's hashtag so that they can thank you properly on social media.

Alphabet rocks

Scatter rocks painted with the letters of the alphabet around the garden. Paint one flat rock or make a waterproof sign: "Can you find the letters of your name? Line them up and leave them out to show that you were here!" You'll want to go out yourself periodically and gather them up to check that you still have a full set. While you're at it, leave a welcoming message for library visitors!

Petrified poetry

Paint rocks with the same kind of words you'd find in a magnetic poetry set (you can find lists online), scatter them about and let the magic happen. Check on it regularly and post pictures in the library or on social media, showcasing visitors' poems "set in stone."

Game pieces

Paint a checkerboard or Tic-Tac-Toe grid on a square of sidewalk. Paint a set of rocks with X's and O's, chess pieces, or just paint half of them red and the other half black to make checkers or Go pieces. How about dominoes? Can you make that work?

Trash to treasure

Reduce waste, foster sustainability, and beautify your surroundings by creating opportunities for customers to transform recycled materials into eye-catching art, which you can hang from the trees and fencing around your building.

Make a weatherproof outdoor sign crediting your customers for their work. (Don't worry, we have tips for making weatherproof signs at the end of this chapter—it's a handy skill to have in your back pocket once you start expanding passive programming beyond the library walls.)

Even the most bright and durable decorations will start to look shabby after being exposed to the elements for a while, so monitor their condition and remove or replace them when appropriate.

Here are a few ideas we like, but there are tons of other projects out there that use recycled objects for crafting outdoor ornaments. We are certain you have the skills to find them.

Water bottle whirligigs

All you need are empty water bottles and permanent markers to create whimsical ornaments that will hang from the trees and spin merrily in the breeze. Invite customers to decorate a bottle with Sharpies and leave it with staff.

Later, you will cut the bottom off the bottle, and starting at the bottom, use scissors to cut a strip about ½" wide. Don't worry if it's not perfect, just keep cutting around and around the bottle to make a spiral, stopping about an inch from the top. Leave the neck and opening intact. The opening functions as a hook for hanging. Hang each whirligig from a separate branch or make a cheerful mobile by looping a bunch of them through a slender branch or dowel that you hang horizontally.

Suncatchers

Collect withdrawn DVDs and invite visitors to decorate them with permanent markers, adhesive jewels, sparkly stickers, mylar, or foil paper. These shiny ornaments not only look festive, but if your library maintains a garden, they'll also scare scavenging birds away!

Use fishing line to hang the suncatchers individually, or cluster them to create a brilliant chandelier effect.

Recycled robots

Plastic bottles and tin cans from the recycling bin transform into friendly droids with the help of aluminum foil, pipe cleaners, googly eyes, and paint pens. Cover the bottle or can with the foil and decorate it. Make a sample robot and set out supplies on a craft table. Ask customers to make one to live in the library garden, and one to take home.

As visitors approach your library, your dazzling art installation will attract their attention. Take advantage of their interest and have an equally eye-catching book display of titles about making art from recycled materials located near the entrance.

Suggested titles:

Dream Something Big by Dianna Hutts Aston
Magic Trash: A Story of Tyree Guyton and His Art by J. H. Shapiro
Kenya's Art by Linda Trice
The Secret Kingdom: Nek Chand, a Changing India, and a Hidden World of Art by Barb Rosenstock
Recycled Crafts Box: Sock Puppets, Cardboard Castles, Bottle Bugs & 37 More Earth-friendly Projects & Activities You Can Create by Laura C. Martin
Recyclables by Anna Llimos Plomer
The Craft-a-Day Book: 30 Projects to Make with Recycled Materials by Kari Cornell
23 Ways to Be an Eco Hero: A Step-by-Step Guide to Creative Ways You Can Save the World by Isabel Thomas

Trash or Treat

At Paula's library, we're always looking for productive ways to encourage our young visitors to burn off energy. After they spend hours and hours sitting in school, some kids are undeniably antsy. At the same time, our library sits on a windy corner that is also a transportation hub. Lots of trash collects in our corners and outside planters. Solution: enlist those energetic kids as litter picker-uppers!

A stash of reusable tote bags and cotton garden gloves are all you'll need to try Trash or Treat. Find an extra recycling bin in which to keep these supplies, and reward successful trash runs with a sticker or a piece of candy. If your library has a button maker, make a bunch of buttons that say "Don't Trash My Library," for rewards with long-term impact.

In the case of this program, rules are extremely important. Type them up, laminate them, and attach a copy to each bag.

1. Stay on the library grounds
2. Don't pick up gross stuff
3. Leaves and sticks stay outside

4. No sharp objects! (broken glass, etc.)

5. Wear your gloves

It's also important to figure out where collected trash should be deposited. You don't want it in the trash can at your desk but sending kids directly to the dumpster isn't safe. Consult with your custodial staff to work out the best place for disposal.

At Paula's library, this passive program has paid off handsomely in terms of awareness, responsibility, and stewardship. Kids who have previously picked up all the trash in the reading garden notice when more trash appears, and spontaneously pick it up and dispose of it properly.

Off the library grounds

Now that you've mastered the art of passive programming in and around your library, take those skills out into the community and think BIG.

Some of the following ideas require a fair amount of planning and work on the back end to pull off, but they can go a long way to help you and your customers better understand and appreciate the community, build relationships between the library and other stakeholders, and draw in new users. We're arguably blurring the lines between programming, outreach and public relations in some cases, so you may want or need to get colleagues from other departments on board to help make these projects happen.

Outreach outpost

Does your library visit local businesses or schools on a regular basis? Perhaps you partner with Libraries without Borders or do storytimes at local barbershops on Saturdays. Give the library a permanent presence at these locations by leaving copies of your activity sheets, instructions for simple crafts that can be done at home, and other passive programming opportunities behind, with directions to bring the completed worksheet or craft to the library in exchange for a small prize.

Little free library

Little Free Libraries differ from your Big Free Library in that they are always open, no library card is needed, and people can return the things they take from it whenever they want to - or not at all. Plus, let's face it, they're adorable.

Install a Little Free Library in front of your building so that customers who stop by after closing don't leave empty handed. Or add one to a Story-Walk or outreach outpost. Stock your Little Free Library with donated books or Advance Reading Copies (ARCs). Your materials selector and people who attend book and library conferences are good sources of ARCs.

Policies regarding the use of withdrawn library books vary from place to place, so check with your powers that be—but if they're cool with it, deleted items get one last chance to find their readers in a Little Free Library.

Be sure your logo and hashtag are prominent—brand the heck out of that Little Free Library so there is no doubt who put it there. Affix a weatherproof sleeve to the side and fill it with flyers advertising library services and programs or stick a pamphlet and library card application inside every book. Members of the community will get a taste of your library's awesomeness, even if they don't yet have a library card.

Go to www.littlefreelibrary.org to learn how to build and start a Little Free Library and add yours to their official map.

Photo contests

Photo contests can piggyback off existing programs like photography workshops, or can stand alone. Refer back to our chapter: Ideas for Anytime for more details about implementing photo contests. Themes that encourage reflection, identification, and community awareness give customers the opportunity to show the world through their eyes.

> A Day in My Life
> What Matters to Me
> The Best Place in Town
> Saturday Afternoon
> Building a Better World
> My Safe Space

I Spy neighborhood adventure

Invite community exploration and awareness with a family activity that also sharpens observation skills. Make a checklist of everyday things one would see while walking around the neighborhood: a squirrel, a stop sign, a mailbox, a green car, a police officer, a person walking a dog, a doctor's office, and so on.

Include pictures of the items on the checklist for pre-readers and offer a small prize when customers return their completed checklist to the library.

StoryWalk

StoryWalks foster family literacy, physical activity, and a love of the great outdoors. Readers of all ages can exercise their minds and bodies by following a set path marked with pages from a picture book. The initial StoryWalk Project was developed by Anne Ferguson of Montpelier, VT in collaboration with the Kellogg-Hubbard Library. It has since been replicated in different ways around the country.

You could do a small-scale StoryWalk inside your library or on the grounds, but setting it up in a public park will broaden awareness of community resources and reach a segment of your population that may not yet be library users.

Select a picture book with wide appeal and a good balance of images and text. Make color copies of the cover and every page of the book, including the title page. Mount each one to a weatherproof sign using the sign-making methods described at the end of this chapter. Based on the book's design and the length of your StoryWalk, it may be necessary to mount a double-paged spread on some signs.

Consider providing a map, or numbering the signs, to ensure they are read in the intended order. Even if you think the sequence is obvious, never underestimate the ability of small children to run in the exact opposite direction as expected or desired.

Include a recursive element and encourage library visits by making a certificate or other token StoryWalkers receive at the end of their walk. They can bring it back to the library for a small prize or entry into a raffle.

Before you reproduce pages of a picture book and post them around town, you absolutely need to contact the publisher for permission. If the publisher has someone in charge of Library Marketing or Library Outreach, and most of the big ones do, we recommend you start with that person as they are likely to respond promptly to your request.

Charleston County Public Library worked with their county Parks and Recreation department to install StoryWalks at the Wannamaker and Palmetto Islands County Parks. The library updates the installations with a new book every quarter. The launch of each new StoryWalk is celebrated with a family event at the park featuring library-led storytimes, activities, and crafts. Participants are given a survey at the end of their walk, which they can return for a chance to win their own copy of the book.

HistoryWalk

For a variation on the StoryWalk, try a HistoryWalk that reveals the effect of time, change, and shifting populations on your community.

The archives of your library and any local museums or historical societies are good sources for finding vintage photos of places around your city or town. With permission, copy these photos and post them on waterproof signs at their original locations, with a bit of descriptive text, to show how buildings and neighborhoods have changed.

Or post the photos in the library and on your website, and challenge people to visit each location and note the differences between then and now. Provide a map and checklist they can bring to the library for a prize or raffle entry after completing the challenge.

Don't forget your library information and logo on anything you post in the community!

Point of view challenge

This is a fun project that challenges you and your community to observe your surroundings from a different perspective and rewards attention to detail.

Go to local landmarks and other well-known places around town and take pictures from unusual points of view, or in some way that the location is not instantly recognizable (a section of the mural in a popular restaurant, the words inscribed over the door to the courthouse, the base of a fountain in the park, etc.). Customers are tasked with identifying the locations from the visual clues provided.

Post the photos inside your library on a bulletin board or monitor, and on your library's website if possible. Offer paper and online entry options, and randomly select a winner from all entries received by the deadline. The owner of that restaurant with the cool mural might be convinced to donate a gift card for your winner in exchange for being included.

Andria's library successfully used this idea to supplement and promote a One Book community reads program. The selected book was photographed at a variety of local sites around town. Staff enjoyed staging the photos as much as customers did identifying them!

Local business scavenger hunt

Support the "shop local" movement, reach new customers, and develop community partnerships with a guided scavenger hunt that sends library users out to explore area stores, restaurants, and coffee shops in search of clues you have left behind.

This is easier to pull off if your city has a "Main Street" or shopping district, and all the participating businesses are within walking distance but could be adapted based on your situation.

Start with a unifying theme. Andria's library has successfully used various summer reading themes as a basis for this activity, which helped promote and generate excitement for that year's program. We have highlighted scientists, musicians, and athletes, but you could do animals, plants, or countries of the world—anything with a diverse range of subjects to pick from will work. Speaking of diversity, if you are featuring people, make sure you represent a variety of races, ages, and cultures.

Design a series of posters, each one featuring a high-resolution image of a different person, place, or thing related to your theme, and a few descriptive sentences about each one. Obviously, all the posters should have the same design, format, and library branding to clearly designate them as part of this program.

Contact local business owners, explain the plan, and invite them to participate. Ask permission to hang your poster in their window or on their community bulletin board for the duration of the program. We recommend a time period of at least two weeks, but a full month is ideal. When you drop off the poster, include a letter explaining the program and the length of time the poster should be displayed, so this information can be shared with all staff.

Create a map showing the locations of participating merchants; on the reverse side, list each business, with a space for participants to write down what they found on each poster. Leave space for their name and contact information. Set a stack of entry forms at each site if possible. Randomly select a winner from all correct entries submitted by the deadline.

Don't forget to hang one of the posters in the library to entice library users to participate, and to draw in new customers who may have first stumbled upon the program by seeing a poster at their favorite ice cream shop.

This "Book on Downtown" program has been wildly popular with families and teens at Andria's library, and most business owners are thrilled to participate as it draws foot traffic and potential new customers to their door at no cost to them. We ask them to donate gift cards or merchandise towards a prize package for the winner, and although they are not required to do so, many happily contribute.

The online world

Online library programming offers parents an additional safe site to send their kids for entertainment and lets the homebound participate in your activities. It can rope people in to try new library features or collections and keeps the library relevant and up to date in people's minds.

You may not have much control over what your library puts online so we're not going to devote a lot of time to this subject, but it is worth exploring the option, especially if your library covers a large geographic area. Look into ways to enhance your online presence, create community, and be responsive.

Could you livestream storytimes, lectures, performances and other library programs, or post recordings of them on your website or social media?

Maybe you can add a section to your website where people can download copies of your mazes, word searches, and other activities. When you produce worksheets, save them as PDFs then convert them to JPEGs, which can be posted to Facebook and other social media sites. You can easily create online versions of your quizzes and polls using Google Forms. Try posting a photo of your guessing jar, along with an online entry form. Be sure to include text reminding customers to visit the library to see the results or to pick up a reward for playing.

Many libraries use Beanstack, ReadSquared, or other software to help users track their progress while participating in reading programs. Surprise! Self-paced reading programs are passive programming too, even if you've never thought of them that way. More and more libraries are offering reading programs in the winter as well as summer—think about using one of these apps to run a small-scale reading incentive program at a nontraditional time. Some of the apps can be modified to award points for any literacy activities you can dream up, such as writing a video game review or following a recipe, or you can stick with the old standby of tracking number of pages read or amount of time spent reading.

Andria's library created a nifty online form where customers can complete a survey of their reading tastes and preferences. Librarians use this information to create a brief, personally curated list of recommended reads, which they send to the user via e-mail.

How to make a quick and easy weatherproof sign

Buy a sheet of corrugated plastic such as Coroplast. This is available at most hardware stores. Use a utility knife to cut the plastic to the desired size. Design your sign using a font type and size that can be easily read from a distance.

Print out your sign and laminate it, or even better, print it directly onto a sheet of transparency film. Glue or staple the transparency or laminated page to the corrugated plastic. Now you have a sign that will stand up to the elements.

Punch holes in your sign and attach it to a tree or fence with zip ties. Or affix a stake and stick it in the ground. Use wood screws to attach it to a wooden fence or furniture; heavy-duty adhesive Velcro or foam mounting tape works with metal or glass.

Note: this sign will be weatherproof for a time, but remember that sun, wind, and rain take a toll on everything eventually. Replace that sign when it starts to show signs of wear.

INSTANT REPLAY:

A 6th grade girl turns in her "Tuesday Newsday" quiz

Me: "Great job! Did you know the answers, or did you look them up?"

Her: "I knew some of them, but had to look up the rest"

Me: "So...maybe you learned something?"

Her: "I learned a LOT of stuff. Our teacher never tells us anything we really need to know."

Me: "Well, that's what the library is for."

11

Passive Programming for Panicky Times

From time to time, libraries must cope with temporary closings due to scheduled renovation or surprise disaster. In 2020 nearly every library in the United States closed its doors and kept them closed for months due to the COVID-19 pandemic. Librarians all over the country scrambled to provide services to our customers and to remain relevant in our communities.

One aspect of that relevance is our role as providers of engaging, entertaining, and educational programming. While many administrators focus on maintaining materials circulation and providing digital reference and resources during library closures, it's important not to let programming fall by the wayside. Lucky you—if you've made it to chapter 11 in this book, you are a passive programming expert, and when the library doors are closed? All programming is passive.

Whether you're operating out of a temporary space, in front of your library, at outreach locations, or in strict isolation, we've got tips and recommendations for implementing passive programming when the building is off-limits.

Be prepared

Some library closures are planned, giving you lots of time to get your distance or off-site programming lined up and ready to go. But some are not. Fire, flood, epidemic, or a direct hit by a meteor—all of these can cause buildings to abruptly close or services to be interrupted with no warning.

Emergencies can knock us a bit off-kilter, and it can be hard to come up with creative new ideas when you're busy coping with a crisis. Keep a stash of ideas ready for a rainy day, and make sure you are positioned to pivot your programming to off-site locations or online.

Maintain a file of ideas

Most of the librarians we know are like squirrels when it comes to program inspirations. Old-school types have manila folders full of scribbled notes, internet printouts, and pages torn from magazines. Nowadays, chances are there are a ton of photos on your phone and at least one Pinterest board. Gen X'ers probably have both.

It is worth getting all these scraps of inspiration together and bundling them into a shareable folder online. At Paula's library, we use Google Drive, but you might use Dropbox, Office 360, or iCloud. When we spent months teleworking during the coronavirus pandemic, having access to that folder of random photos, screenshots, and pdfs jumpstarted the idea process even when our brains were foggy with stress.

Build relationships with relevant staff

Your system's social media coordinator is going to be your best friend if you end up going all digital with your programming. The "there's an app for that" person in your IT department can save you a lot of time if you find yourself looking for the best way to present programs online. And it does not hurt to have a good relationship with the person who has to approve everything that goes on the website. Does your system have a blog? Who's in charge of the blog?

Figure out who those people are, and make friends. We're not saying bake 'em a pie (although baked goods are a cherished library tradition when currying favor), but make contact.

- **Recruit that IT person as a collaborator**—"Hey we've been using Kahoot for our trivia contest; do you have any advice about other apps we could use?"
- **Write some blog posts.**
- **Ask the social media gatekeeper what formats and file sizes they prefer** when pushing content to Twitter, Instagram, Facebook, or YouTube. Become a frequent contributor, sending pictures and videos that they don't have to edit or convert.
- **Write captions, descriptions, or tweets yourself.** Even if a more marketing-oriented person ends up rewriting them, they'll appreciate not having to chase you down to ask for names or dates. This will speed your posts through the approval process as well.
- **Never, *ever* forget to follow your institution's rules on media releases.**

This way, if and when online outlets become your only way of connecting with your customers, that IT person will be ready and willing to work with you if you abruptly have to figure out screencasting or you want to try hosting a real-time quiz. The blog person will look to you to write a post. Your social media people will already trust you to provide quality content, and your path to approval will be shortened.

Assess what is available to you

The COVID-19 crisis was ridiculously challenging—not only were our buildings closed to the public and in many cases staff, but contact with our customers was not allowed, and group gatherings were completely out of the question. Where are you working during your emergency?

- **In a planned alternate location.** When libraries close for planned renovation, often they operate on a limited basis at another location. Remember, if you've got a wall, you've got a space for passive programming.
- **Mobile services or outreach locations.** If there is no alternative space, are you using mobile services (bookmobiles, mobile job centers, etc.) or setting up at outreach locations? This is often the only option when disasters such as storm damage or fire strike.
  - If your physical space is constrained, can you hand out craft kits or activity sheets along with other services?
  - If you are doing regularly scheduled outreach at a school, rec center, or senior center, is there a centrally located bulletin board you can ask to commandeer for the duration of your disaster?
- **The outside of your building.** Can you get into the building, even if customers can't? Look at your building's envelope—windows are wonderful spaces for messages, overhangs can support banners or shelter a noticeboard, and lawns or landscaped areas can sport signs of all kinds.
- **Online—or not.** In all of the above situations, your friend the Internet is also available (see below). Unless of course the disaster is some kind of global EMP or a complete breakdown of the power grid. We're writing in Spring of 2020, so at this point it would feel foolish to rule anything out. So. In the case of a global EMP, a complete breakdown of the power grid, or, who knows, the Moon exploding, your best bet is to tear up all those activity sheets and make them available to your customers for use as toilet paper. If we've learned one thing from the COVID-19 crisis, it's that there's never enough toilet paper.

Adapt your existing passive programming

Once you've figured out what avenues are available, look at your slate of planned passive programs or programs that you have implemented successfully in the past. Which can be tweaked to work in a window? In a bookmobile? Online?

Writing and drawing prompts

Almost any service point, even short-term outreach locations like laundromats and supermarkets, can include a topical or fun writing or drawing prompt. If you don't have access to a bulletin board or whiteboard, bring roll paper and tape it to a wall. If you're working outside or in a large space like a gym, bring an easel and a flip pad.

If you're limited to online interaction, you can post your prompts as social media or blog posts. Invite customers to respond in the comments or to post on their own social media with a hashtag.

Photo prompts

Here's something that you can't easily do on a whiteboard – ask customers to respond to a prompt with a photo. You may have seen examples of this on Facebook: "Post the 4th picture on your camera roll" or, "Post a picture of something yellow." Try a more topical or library-oriented prompt like, "Share your work-from-home setup."

Leave a message

One of our favorite prompts is 100% open ended. "What would you like to say to the community?" On a whiteboard, bulletin board, roll paper, chalk, or using painted rocks—invite customers to leave a message of friendship or hope outside the library. Especially in times of crisis, giving people permission and space to express themselves demonstrates respect and compassion.

Sample prompts

- What do you miss about the library?
- What's your favorite hobby?
- Give us some good advice for coping with this crisis
- Post a picture of the pet who's happy you're spending more time at home.
- Recommend a great series (TV or book)

Polls and voting

Polls and voting are even easier. Post your question on an easel, roll paper or a board, and mark out areas for people to vote with a sticker or marker. Be sure to use a yardstick to make your lines straight, or washi tape if you have some. If you have a table at your service point, conduct a two-option poll with two jars and a bowl of checkers or other small items to use as ballots—even dry beans will do in a pinch!

Polls and voting can even work on a sidewalk or garden space outside the library. Post your question on a sign or paint it on the sidewalk and put out two buckets and a supply of small stones—or mark off sections of sidewalk. Check in on this station every day or so—you'll want to post the results to social media. Besides, the stones will scatter and you'll need to resupply.

Twitter and other social media platforms make it easy to create online polls. Or use Google Forms or an app like SurveyMonkey to collect answers. Be sure to announce the results in a separate post!

Sample questions

- What color should the chairs in the new reading lounge be?
- I agree with the Mayor's decision to _____ (Yes/No)

Contests and quizzes

Activities that require detailed feedback, whether in the form of answers or judging, take a little more time to set up. If you're working at a temporary, mobile, or outreach site, type up your quiz, print it, and distribute as usual. But if you're in a no-contact situation, you're probably limited to online presentation.

Quizzes

GOOGLE FORMS

It is super easy to set up a news or trivia quiz using Google Forms. This is a satisfying format for the user, too, as they can see not only their results but how

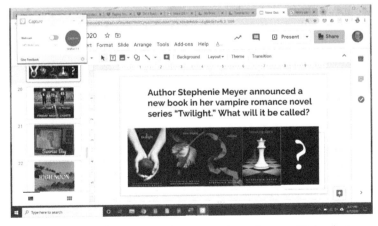

Using Google Slides and a screencast program to make a multiple-choice current events quiz.

many other people got each question right or wrong. Post a link to the form on your library's social media or in a post on your library's web page.

PRERECORDED VIDEO

Paula's department presented their weekly news quiz for kids as a screencast video. The multiple-choice questions (with picture hints) were typed into a slideshow, which staff narrated while recording their voice and the slideshow using a screencasting app (we used TechSmith Capture). Our videos included the answers and an explanation at the end, but you might try recording the answers as a separate video to be posted the next day or week.

LIVE EVENT

We know of several live online trivia nights hosted by libraries across the country. These interactive events are not technically passive programming, so we're going to sidle off away from here mumbling something about the fact that technology in this area is moving so quickly anything we said about it would be obsolete in a month anyway. Chances are someone in IT has been *dying* to try something like this. This is their chance to shine!

Guessing/estimation

A big, colorful estimation jar is a visually magnetic item at any service point, especially at an outreach event. Ask for an e-mail address or phone number on the estimation slip so that you can share the results with everyone who made a guess. While you're at it, send links to your library's landing page for digital resources.

In a no-touch situation, place your estimation jar in a window or on a table in a glass vestibule. It's still a cool thing to look at, and great for passing the time if your customers (or their kids) are stuck waiting for sidewalk service. Post the answer on a covered card or include an estimation slip as a bookmark when you deliver their hold materials.

A variation on this is to cover a window with (removable) stickers. Spell out "How many dots (or stars or hearts or whatever you're using)?" Passersby *could* count them all, but some will use the opportunity to practice their math skills or pass those skills on to another.

Photo and art contests

If your building closure has resulted in an increase in your online programming, why not try a community art show? Many social media platforms incorporate a feedback channel in the form of comments, shares, and/or hashtags. Coordinate with your social media gatekeeper to devise the best strategy for an online contest.

Activity sheets

Save as PDF or JPG

When you produce activity sheets, save them as PDFs then convert them to JPEGs, which can be posted to Facebook and other social media sites. In Word, use "Save as" on the File menu to save your file as a PDF, or select "Print to PDF" from the Print menu. PDFs are more easily shareable online than doc files. JPGs are even better—they can be shared via Facebook, text, and WhatsApp. Use an online converter app or, in a pinch, take a picture of the printed document with your phone.

If you use an online puzzle maker program to make word searches, mazes, or crosswords, look through all of the print and save options carefully. Chances are, you will find Print to PDF or Save as JPEG—and if not, try a different puzzle maker website.

Get in the habit of making a PDF or JPG version of all your activity sheets. Keep those files in your ideas folder for a rainy day.

Share online

Work with your website coordinator to see if you can add a section to your website where people can download copies of your mazes, word searches, and other activities. Try posting a photo of your guessing jar, along with an online entry form. Be sure to include text reminding customers to visit the library to see the results or to pick up a reward for playing.

Use your windows

Any activity challenge that you can post on a bulletin board will work in a window too. Match games, find the pairs, spot the difference, I Spy, and even mazes can be created using construction paper and taped in the window.

A programmable cutter such as a Cricut makes this much easier, but if you don't have one, don't despair. Look for precut shapes, removable stickers, or even light objects such as ping-pong balls, crayons, or tissue paper flowers.

When customers notice your colorful window challenges they'll detour out of their way to pass by and will be more likely to notice when your doors are open again.

Reading challenges

Many libraries use Beanstack, ReadSquared, or other software to help users track their progress while participating in reading programs. Self-paced reading programs are great passive programs that keep customers engaged with the library. More and more libraries are offering reading programs in the winter as well as summer—think about using one of these apps to run a small-scale reading incentive program at a nontraditional time.

Some of the apps can be customized to award points for any literacy activities you can dream up, such as writing a video game review or following a recipe, or you can stick with the old standby of tracking number of pages read or amount of time spent reading.

Distance reader advisory

Maintaining a personal relationship with customers can be tough when the library is closed. Most libraries offer reference service via phone or chat, but in our experience, customers rarely use that service to solicit recommendations. Finding a way to offer reader advisory service even when you're closed helps guarantee that your customers will be back once you reopen.

VIA E-MAIL

Andria's library created a nifty online form where customers can complete a survey of their reading tastes and preferences. Librarians use this information to create a brief, personally curated list of recommended reads, which we send to the user via e-mail.

VIA VIDEO

At Paula's library, we solicited the same type of information via a Facebook post. Several queries were bundled together into a recorded video response during which Paula (and her son) recommended books and series based on each reader profile.

In conclusion: Active passive programming

Well, hello, contradiction in terms! During a crisis or building emergency, up is down, outside is inside, and even your active programming is likely to be passive. While libraries were closed during the COVID-19 pandemic, we were blown away by the variety of ways that library staff used their talents, tech savvy, homes, pets, and even family members to present distance programming.

We saw staff members use Zoom to conduct Teen Advisory Group meetings; we witnessed staff organize game tournaments using Discord seemingly overnight; we saw recorded storytimes and Zoom storytimes and storytimes on Facebook Live. Customers benefited from videos on guided meditation and how to apply for unemployment benefits. Library staff presented cooking programs; craft demonstrations; booktalks; and special content related to Women's History Month, Asian Pacific American Heritage Month, and, when the country rose up in protest over the death of George Floyd and too many others, racism, and the civil rights movement.

It was amazing and inspiring.

However, we also saw library systems delay putting storytimes online until they caught up with Everything You Always Needed to Know about Copyright and Fair Use. In systems with little previous experience with teleworking, we saw HR departments throwing webinars on how to use Zoom, Blackboard, WebEx, and other tools at us in a desperate attempt to get everyone up and running with distance collaboration. In the worst cases, we heard about systems playing a quick, panicky game of Who Knows the YouTube Password?

Don't be that guy.

Keeping yourself educated on developments in the library world is part of being prepared for emergency. So is maintaining good relationships throughout your system, especially in the technical and online areas. But most of all, exercising your programming muscles, especially those nimble, reflexive passive programming muscles, is the best way to keep your mind open to innovative solutions and slivers of opportunity, no matter what the world throws at you.

Appendix

Resources

What we've offered in this book is just a starting point. Keep your eyes and your mind open, and you will find ideas for passive programs in any number of places.

- Schools
- Museums
- Other libraries
- Grocery stores
- The mall
- Conferences
- State or county fair
- Kids page in the newspaper
- Activity pages in children's magazines

Take a picture so that you don't have to rely on your memory!

Online, we keep tabs on a couple of Facebook groups: Programming Librarians, Teen Librarian's Toolbox, and our state library groups. Follow the hashtag #passiveprogramming on Instagram or Pinterest and see what turns up.

General resources

Materials

Basic supplies

Many items on this list (none of which is absolutely required to do effective passive programming) are stock items from your usual office or craft supply vendor. Some are harder to find, and in some cases, quality varies widely from brand to brand. In those cases, recommended sources and brands are noted.

- Giant coloring sheets: Stuff2Color offers a variety.
- Vinyl stickers: custom or preprinted.

- Clips: Bulldog clips and binder clips work just fine in most cases. Cheap plastic or wooden clothespins are a more festive choice.
- Thumbtacks
- Magnetic clips
- Dot magnets for voting: The two-sided dot magnets from Magnatag are available in a range of sizes and come in affordable sets of 25.
- Dot stickers for voting (large and small): Avery makes a variety of sizes and colors.
- Bulletin board border
- Painters tape
- Washi tape
- Clear shipping tape
- Whiteboard markers
- Magnetic whiteboard markers: if you can't find the kind with a magnet attached, glue a magnet on with hot glue.
- Chalk markers: if you're writing on windows, these easily removable opaque markers are a must. Chalktastic, Chalkola, and Crafty Croc are brands that get high marks.
- Construction paper
- Glue: we swear by Tacky Glue for its hold, quick setting time, and easy cleanup.
- Sidewalk chalk

For some supplies, such as whiteboard markers, we keep two sets. The "good" whiteboard markers live in a box at the desk for drawing our whiteboard prompts, and the "other" set is available for customers to use. When one of the "good" markers begins to lose some juice, or if its tip gets mushy or frayed, it becomes an "other" marker.

Beyond the basics

- Plastic eggs.
- Roll paper: Pay attention to the dimensions when ordering. We have mistakenly ended up with a roll so large it couldn't be lifted or rolls so slender we needed three just to complete one project.
- Transparency film: Generally cheaper than craft plastic, but flimsier, too.
- Velcro dots.
- Art tissue.
- Sign holders: Whether you use Lucite display stands from your library supplier, pole-mounted signs, or magnetic sign holders, sign holders are a must to give your signs, lists, and instructions more authority.
- Plastic bins.

- Flip pads.
- Dot markers: The most durable sponge-top markers we've found are marketed as "bingo daubers" and are available online or at big box stores. Or stop in at your local bingo parlor!
- Adhesive gems.
- Floor stickers: Due to social distancing, durable graphics that stick to low pile carpet or smooth flooring have become easier to find. You can even find stickers that work on asphalt or concrete. They do have to be custom ordered, however. Search on "carpet decals" or "floor stickers."
- Discarded books and magazines.

Natural materials

- Sticks
- Rocks
- Autumn leaves
- Pine cones

Give natural materials 48 hours in a freezer or 10 seconds in the microwave in order to render harmless any wee beasties that may have traveled inside with them.

Equipment

- Oversized egg timer.
- Giant six-sided die.
- Button maker: Button maker machines are one-size-fits-one. Double check that the machine you are looking at makes buttons in a size that will work for you before ordering and when you order blanks and supplies make sure that the dimensions match your machine!
- Bypass paper cutter: Whether you opt for a light and cheap model like a Swingline or a heavy and durable machine like the X-Acto Commercial Grade Trimmer (drool!), look into how the manufacturer recommends keeping the blade sharp. A dull paper cutter is just a really big paperweight.
- Die-cut machine: Ask around—your system may already own an Accu-Cut or Ellison machine or one of the newer programmable die-cut machines like a Cricut or Silhouette. Check online reviews before you invest.
- A/V cart.
- Book cart.
- Easels.

Surface treatments

Magnetic primer: You will need multiple coats of this paint, regardless of the brand, and it doesn't wash out well, so you'll need disposable brushes and rollers.

Chalkboard paint: Rust-Oleum Flat Black Chalkboard Paint yields good results with just two coats.

Dry erase paint: IdeaPaint is the high-end brand of dry erase paint, and Rust-Oleum and Krylon make versions too. We have heard success stories and disappointment stories about all of these products.

Dry erase contact paper: For smaller areas, you might try peel and stick dry erase film. There are many brands, including ThinkBoard, Post-It, Kassa, and Canvix. Every brand we've tried sticks much better to tables and other horizontal surfaces than on walls, but taping around the edges improves adhesion dramatically. Humidity and surface texture will affect this material's ability to stay put.

Online

Puzzle-maker offers a wide variety of customizable pencil puzzles. https://www.puzzle-maker.com/

The Playworks Game Library is well worth exploring for ideas you might adapt to your library and your customers. https://www.playworks.org/game-library/

http://www.holidayscalendar.com/ Great for the inclusion of observances and holidays around the world. How are you planning to celebrate Kazakh Unity Day on May 1? Cross your t's by checking http://www.holidayinsights.com/moreholidays/ as well.

Books

As a last-ditch seat-of-the-pants maneuver, we've been known to make color copies of pencil puzzles or I Spy puzzles from books and make them available as passive program activities. This is great for unannounced school visits. Look for books from Windmill Books, Lerner Publications, and Capstone.

Resources for specific activities

Mazes

Look for books by Roxie Munro, Sean Jackson, or try mazegenerator.net.

Current events and pop culture quizzes

Look for weekly news quizzes online. Adapt what you find to fit your library community, make it multiple choice, make the questions easier (or harder!), add a picture hint, and make a decision about how grim you want to go.

KET (Kentucky Educational Television) has a weekly news quiz for students. The Google or PDF form of that quiz is easily adapted. KET also posts a weekly opinion question that makes a great prompt or poll. https://www .ket.org/education/newsquiz/

The New York Times also posts a weekly news quiz (although it suspends for the summer months). This content can be simplified for kids or used as-is for teens and adults. https://www.nytimes.com/column/learning-news-quiz

Time Magazine, the BBC, Slate, and the PBS program Washington Week also post weekly news quizzes.

If the news is just too depressing for civilized use, fill your Newsday gap with a pop culture quiz. Check Buzzfeed, hwdyk.com (How Well Do You Know?), and VOYA magazine's teen pop culture quiz (http://voyamagazine.com /tags/teen-pop-culture-quiz/). Or just google "trivia for kids" and you'll find a wealth of resources.

Word searches

There are a number of custom word search generators online. We like Puzzle-maker (http://puzzlemaker.discoveryeducation.com/) in part because it has a filter that automatically eliminates randomly created "offensive words."

Look for generators that create puzzles that print gracefully, like thewordsearch.com or ABCya (https://www.abcya.com/games/make_a_word _search) or that offer fun puzzle shapes, as mywordsearch.com/ does.

Languages

Omniglot

Omniglot (/www.omniglot.com) is a comprehensive resource on writing systems and languages. You will find written alphabets for world languages, including alphabets no longer in use (you'll have at least three choices if you do Write Your Name in Runic) as well as many more fictional languages than you probably knew existed. Wakandan, Dothraki, Klingon, Aurebesh, and Na'vi are all in there.

Native languages are also well represented on Omniglot, as are communication systems for people with communication, language, and learning disabilities. The Multilingual Phrase Finder uses an input and output drop-down menu to translate dozens of phrases into any of 300 languages all at once. By and large, this site can be your first stop when working up any Say Hi, Write Your Name or other language program.

Other language resources

Native Languages (http://www.native-languages.org/): A rather bare bones website that has been around for a long time and includes links to an immense amount of information on over 800 languages.

Your name in Akan (Ghanaian): https://thisworldmusic.com/african-day -name-generator/.

Hello in 100 languages (doesn't include the Americas): https://bilingua.io/how -to-say-hello-in-100-languages.

Saying hello in Native American languages: https://www.powwows.com/how -to-say-hello/.

Reading, listening, and writing related

Book awards

Find lists of recipients of every award and honor given by the **American Library Association** on their website (http://www.ala.org/awardsgrants /awards/browse/bpma).

The **American Indian Youth Literature Award** was first awarded in 2006. Find all award and honor recipients at https://ailanet.org/activities /american-indian-youth-literature-award/.

The **Asian/Pacific American Award for Literature** honors books for children, young adults, and adults. Find all past winners here: http://www.apalaweb .org/awards/literature-awards/.

The website of the **Booker Prize** has an irritating scroll-by-year interface, but all their winners are listed: https://thebookerprizes.com/fiction/backlist /2020.

Winners of **The Edgars**, awarded by the Mystery Writers of America, are in a tidy database: http://theedgars.com/awards/.

Winners of the **Hugo Awards** for science fiction are listed at http://www .thehugoawards.org/hugo-history/.

All winners of the **National Book Awards** are here: https://www.nationalbook .org/national-book-awards/years/.

Past winners of the **RITA Award** for distinction in romance fiction are listed here: https://www.rwa.org/Online/Online/Awards/RITA_Awards/Past _RITA_Winners.aspx.

A full list of all recipients of the **Sydney Taylor Book Award** is available as a PDF on the Jewish Library Association's website: https://jewishlibraries .starchapter.com/images/downloads/Sydney_Taylor_Book_Award/stba _quick_list.pdf.

Reading challenges

Book Riot https://bookriot.com/2019/12/03/2020-read-harder-challenge/
PopSugar https://www.popsugar.com/entertainment/reading-challenge-2020 -46857621
The Rory Gilmore Reading Challenge https://www.listchallenges.com/rory -gilmore-reading-challenge

Poetry

Poetry challenges are offered by Poets & Writers (https://www.pw.org/content /poetry_challenge), Writers Digest (https://www.writersdigest.com/poetry -challenge-2020), or try the free Daily Prompt app.
Poets.org has an updated 30 Ways to Celebrate National Poetry Month, including 30 activities for the virtual or online classroom (or library!): https://poets.org/national-poetry-month/30-ways-celebrate-national -poetry-month.
Library of Congress has a huge collection of poetry on audio: https://www.loc .gov/rr/program/bib/poetryaudio/.

Letter-writing campaigns

Support Our Troops https://supportourtroops.org/cards-letters
Operation Gratitude https://www.operationgratitude.com/express-your -thanks/write-letters/
Care Letters of Hope https://www.care.org/get-involved/letters-hope
Letters of Love https://letters-of-love.org/
Save the Children https://www.savethechildren.org/us/about-us/become -a-partner/corporations/employee-engagement/letter-writing

Hard-to-find facts

Weather records

Current Results is a website with weather and science facts and is a useful source of records and counts. The author cites her sources—this gets a big thumbs' up from us librarians! https://www.currentresults.com/Weather -Extremes/

Get information about local weather extremes from NOAA. https://w2
.weather.gov/climate/local_data.php

Temperature and precipitation averages and extremes for U.S. cities and states.
http://coolweather.net/

Facts about Africa

African countries in order of date of independence: https://www.thoughtco
.com/chronological-list-of-african-independence-4070467

African languages by country, along with some notes: https://www
.nationsonline.org/oneworld/african_languages.htm

Famous folks

Lists of famous people with a particular cultural, religious, or ethnic background are not as easy to find as you might think. Sometimes Wikipedia seems
like the only option. Here are some sources we've found in our deep dives into
important people. When possible, we have used lists compiled by people who
identify as a member of the group.

African Americans: Hard to argue with the Undefeated 44, a list "of 44
Blacks who shook up the world or at least their corner of it" (https://
theundefeated.com/features/the-undefeated-44-most-influential-black
-americans-in-history/). Look to *The Root* for a current list of young
innovators and leaders (https://interactives.theroot.com/root-100-2019/).
And a great roundup of lists of notable African Americans appears on the
University of Illinois Extension's Black History Month page (https://web
.extension.illinois.edu/bhm/notable.html)

Arab Americans: The Islamic Networks Group has a list of scientist, politi-
cians, entertainers, and writers of Arab descent. https://ing.org/national
-arab-american-heritage-month/.

Asian Americans: The Goldhouse A100 List honors achievers in business and
culture https://goldhouse.org/a100/?y=2020.

Jewish people: You could do worse than to consult the list of notable American Jews put together by Geni https://www.geni.com/projects/Notable
-American-Jews/7296.

Latinx people: Finding one list of notable Latinx people isn't easy. We tend to
pull from this *Time Magazine* list (http://content.time.com/time/specials
/packages/completelist/0,29569,2008201,00.html) and this slightly outdated list of influential Latinos from 2017 put out by *Latino Leaders Magazine* (https://www.latinoleadersmagazine.com/julyaugust-2017/2018/6/20
/the-101-most-influential-latinos). Infoplease also has a long, useful list
(https://www.infoplease.com/notable-hispanic-americans-z).

American Muslims: This CNN list is good (https://www.cnn.com/interactive /2018/05/us/influential-muslims/), augmented by this shockingly brief one from *Biography Online* (https://www.biographyonline.net/people/famous /muslims.html).

Native Americans: *Biography* has a list (https://www.biography.com/people /groups/native-american) as does Infoplease (https://www.infoplease.com /people/famous-native-americans). This list from *Partnership with Native Americans* (http://www.nativepartnership.org/site/PageServer?pagename= pwna_native_biographies) covers mainly historical figures.

Supplies for special spaces

Listening

Listening center: Many libraries have disused listening center supplies gathering dust. Look around for existing equipment or purchase from your library or school supplier. The newest ones eliminate cords by using Bluetooth connections.

Listening chair: Your best bet for a dedicated listening center chair with built-in speakers or a headphone jack is a chair purpose-built for gaming. As of this writing, library suppliers have yet to offer gaming chairs, so read reviews in order to find the most durable and flexible option for your library.

Chill zone

Ambient noise machine: These range from simple machines with a single sound option ('LectroFan, Dohm, Snooz) to fancy items loaded with sounds, nightlights, and even a baby monitor (Hatch Baby Rest). This last one might be a nice option for keeping tabs on what's going on in your Chill Zone.

Filtered lighting: Fluorescent light filters are available from educational and specialty suppliers. You can buy plain or patterned panels or filters that slide directly onto the light tubes. Brands and suppliers include Octo Lights, Educational Insights, and Naturalux.

Buddha Board: These paint-with-water boards are available at a variety of price points.

Yoga or qi gong poster: The website *Kids Yoga Stories* (https://www .kidsyogastories.com/) offers free downloadable posters that are attractive and cleanly designed. Grand Basics sells large, gym-quality laminated post- ers of yoga poses, stretches, and more.

Meditation apps: Headspace, Calm, Aura, and SimpleHabit are some apps that we have found to be effective. Read reviews to find the latest and best for your Chill Zone. SmilingMind and Stop, Breathe, and Think are good for children.

Photo booth

Lightbox (tabletop studio): These range in price from about $40 to nearly $200. Look for a kit that includes a translucent photo tent, onboard lights or light stands, and interchangeable backgrounds. Some are foldable for easy storage. Available from B&H Photo.

Tripods and clamps: Look for a phone stand with a tripod base or a base that clamps securely to a tabletop or shelf using a screw—spring-loaded clips are not secure or durable enough for public use. Also available from B&H Photo.

Stop motion animation apps: As of this writing, Stop Motion Studio, Funmotion, and PicPac lead the pack. But free stop motion animation apps are abundant. Read reviews or download and experiment until you find the best apps to load on a library tablet.

Nature Nook

Window-mounted bird feeder: Look for sturdy acrylic, strong suction cups, and an easily refillable birdseed tray. Products by Nature-Gear and Perky-Pet receive high marks.

Resources for outside experiences

Weatherproof sign materials

Coroplast is made up of two sheets of plastic with a shallow layer of perpendicular cells sandwiched in between—it resembles corrugated cardboard made of plastic. This strong, light, weatherproof material is available by the sheet at hardware stores, box suppliers, and Uline. Other brand names include Plaskolite and Stratocore.

H-stands, the wire stands frequently used to hold up yard signs, are inexpensive and readily available. They work well with lightweight signs and last a few months.

Little free libraries

Plans, maps, and installation tips are available on the littlefreelibrary.org website.

Bibliography

Alessio, Amy J., and Kimberly A. Patton. *A Year of Programs for Teens 2*. American Library Association, 2011.

Alexander, Linda B., and Nahyun Kwon. *Multicultural Programs for Tweens and Teens*. American Library Association, 2010.

Bangsbo, Jens, et al. "The Copenhagen Consensus Conference 2016: Children, Youth, and Physical Activity in Schools and during Leisure Time." *British Journal of Sports Medicine*, vol. 50, no. 19, 2016, pp. 1177–1178, doi:10.1136/bjsports-2016-096325.

Banks, Carrie Scott, and Cindy Mediavilla. *Libraries & Gardens: Growing Together*. ALA Editions, 2019.

Barrett, Peter, et al. "The Impact of Classroom Design on Pupils' Learning: Final Results of a Holistic, Multi-Level Analysis." *Building and Environment*, vol. 89, 2015, pp. 118–133, doi:10.1016/j.buildenv.2015.02.013.

Connery, Dianne. "Webinar: Growing Your Library's Role: Creating a Community Garden with Impact." *Programming Librarian*, 2 May 2018, programminglibrarian.org/learn /growing-your-librarys-role-creating-community-garden-impact.

Fernandes, Myra A., et al. "The Surprisingly Powerful Influence of Drawing on Memory." *Current Directions in Psychological Science*, vol. 27, no. 5, 2018, pp. 302–308, doi:10 .1177/0963721418755385.

Gronneberg, Janet, and Sam Johnston. "7 Things You Should Know About Universal Design for Learning." *Educause*, 6 Apr. 2015, library.educause.edu/resources/2015/4/7-things -you-should-know-about-universal-design-for-learning.

Honnold, RoseMary. *More Teen Programs That Work*. Neal-Schuman, 2005.

Honnold, RoseMary. *101+ Teen Programs That Work*. Neal-Schuman, 2003.

Lenstra, Noah. "THINKING OUTSIDE OF THE STACKS: The Growth of Nature Smart Libraries." *Children & Nature Network*, 8 July 2019, www.childrenandnature.org/2019 /06/20/thinking-outside-of-the-stacks-the-growth-of-nature-smart-libraries/.

"Libraries as Nature Connectors." *Cities Connecting Children to Nature*, National League of Cities and Children and Nature Network, www.childrenandnature.org/wp-content /uploads/CCCN_NatureLibraries.pdf.

LittleFreeLibrary. *Little Free Library*, littlefreelibrary.org/.

Nanney, Emily, et al. "Webinar: Taking a Walk with the Library: StoryWalk®, Walking Book Clubs and More." *Programming Librarian*, American Library Association, 15

Apr. 2020, programminglibrarian.org/learn/taking-walk-library-storywalk%C2%AE
-walking-book-clubs-and-more.

Ott, Valerie A. *Teen Programs with Punch: A Month-by-Month Guide*. Libraries Unlimited, 2006.

Owens, Maggie. "The Sweet Science of Shipping." *Fandom*, 10 July 2018, www.fandom.com /articles/shipping-characters-sweet-science.

Pelczar, M., et al. "Public Libraries Survey 2017." *Institute of Museum and Library Services*, 20 Feb. 2020, www.imls.gov/research-evaluation/data-collection/public-libraries -survey.

Peterson, Kay, et al. "Moving and Learning." *Journal of Experiential Education*, vol. 38, no. 3, 26 June 2014, pp. 228–244, doi:10.1177/1053825914540836.

Reid, Ian. "The 2017 Public Library Data Service Report: Characteristics and Trends." Edited by Carl Thompson, *Public Libraries Online. The 2017 Public Library Data Service Report: Characteristics and Trends Comments*, Public Library Association, 2017, publiclibrariesonline.org/2017/12/the-2017-public-library-data-service-report -characteristics-and-trends/.

Schadlich, Megan Emery. *Cooking up Library Programs Teens and 'Tweens Will Love: Recipes for Success*. Libraries Unlimited, 2015.

Wichman, Emily T. *Librarian's Guide to Passive Programming: Easy and Affordable Activities for All Ages*. Libraries Unlimited, 2012.

Index

About the Authors

Paula Willey is a children's librarian in Baltimore, Maryland. She is the author of countless reviews and articles for publications such as *School Library Journal*, the *Baltimore Sun*, and *Booklist*, and is a speaker on such topics as book illustration, trends in children's literature, and what it means when a kid is totally into truly creepy books. Her whiteboard game is tight.

Andria L. Amaral has spent over 20 years planning and developing public library programs, collections, and services for students in grades 6–12. She has provided professional development workshops and moderated panels at library and education conferences such as PLA and NCTE, has been a guest lecturer to MLIS students at the University of South Carolina and YA literature students at the College of Charleston, and serves on the board of the YALLFest young adult literature festival. She lives in Charleston, South Carolina, with her husband and pack of rescue dogs.